Thank you especially to Dallas but *especially* Eric for proofing this nonsense and gassing me up with compliments. It helped a lot.

Oh, and to Eric for encouraging me to give up teaching on a whim in Annamaria's Creative Writing class. It all worked out.

And to Annamaria and Jamii for making me a better writer, even if it took a long time to shake itself out.

And to K for encouraging me to try to be kinder to people, even when I want to be a real asshole just for old time's sake.

This is exciting for me. I finally finished a project.

THE TWO DEVILS ON MY SHOULDERS

I never sold my soul
But I got two devils tellin' me what to do
Their names are Apathy and Anger
They are saying things

They ain't whispering sweet nothin's

COYOTE WOMAN

I recall, with fondness and chagrin,
My father's favorite yarn
about the Coyote Woman
who lived in an abandoned barn.
He used it as a weapon
when I was on a tear,
if I could not behave
he'd surely take me there.
Three quarters of a mile
From the front door of our home,
on the north side of the road
lived this creature of Moreau.
Of course I never saw her,
but my dad still insists
Coyote Woman lived there,
so this memory persists.
We never really settled
on how she would appear
but when I was misbehaving
I felt that she was near.
Was she just a woman?
Who controlled the pack?
Or maybe not a human,
A beast with hair upon her back?
Were there fangs dripping,
with blood from boys like me?
How much of her was canine?
I guess we'll never see.
They razed the barn in August
Of my 16th year.
Unceremoniously burning
my childhood's biggest fear.
With her died my goblin
and took away my Hell
if Coyote Woman can't hurt me
then nothing ever will.

A VERY UGLY MAN

He has a face
That looks just like a shoe
If you threw that shoe in acid
Then let Fido have a chew
Tossed it down the stairs
Stomped it in the mud
Then drug it through the graveyard
And shot it with a gun
His breath is simply ghastly
It'll kill you where you stand
Wilt your heart like flowers
Cook you like a pan
He smells like a hunk of meat
That was left out in the sun
He packs a fiery wallop
His smell weighs a metric ton
His eyes appear like saucers
If they shattered on the floor
Then got swept up like garbage
And tossed out the front door
His stomach is a bay window
With panoramic views
His indigestion lethal
Worse than Germany with Jews

A metaphor, not racism
Although it is rather crass
But WW2 is Christmas time
Compared to his baggy ass
His flatulence is morbid
It coats with gnarly funk
And if you chance to smell it
You'd rather mate a skunk
They say it was an asteroid
That slew the giant brutes
But we all know what happened
The lizards sniffed his toots
His feet are reminiscent
Of snakes in throes of love
His mangled toes are yellowed
Assured never to be rubbed
His personality is poison
His words are just a hiss
Short and often flaccid
Like the dick with which he'll piss
If you should happen upon him
Please, go the other way
His appearance surely frightens men
And turns the ladies gay!

A MOST UGLY WOMAN

She isn't truly fat
Or particularly rotund
It's just that everything is flat
Amongst a couple hund
Her face looks like a pancake
Her chest looks like the floor
Her nose looks like she ran headfirst
Into an oaken door
Her most impressive feature
Is when you look away
And never mind her ashen skin
She's a sooty, crusty gray
Her fingers are yellowed
From smoking GPCs
Her legs are short and stubby
Bowing at the knees
Her ass looks like a horse's
That's been turned into glue
And if you tanned her leathered face
It would make a proper shoe
Her expression is distressing
Like she's chewing broken glass
Her voice is a wood chipper
Instead of logs, it's chopping cats
Animalistic screeching
Turns whitest milk to curd
Coupled with her smoker's hack
And dripping nasally words
Don't even think of licking
Upon her nether bits

Unless you are a masochist
Or are fond of tasting shit
Certainly a base comparison
But I don't feel disgrace
You'll know why it's perfect
If you stuff manure in your face
Back to our dame in question
To kiss her is to die
Not from red hot passion
Instead from ocher eye
If she was Bob Ross's painting
She'd have a happy little boil
If she were a homeless
She'd have clothing, extra soiled
Hideous in spirit
The quintessential witch
If you saw her in person
You'd beat yourself with switch
Her breath, frighteningly caustic
It empties out a room
Beware of her surroundings
She's never touched a broom
She makes the Grinch look friendly
She turns depression glad
Not because she's charming
But because you aren't so bad
If you chance to meet her
Turn quickly, run for home!
She makes gay ladies long for dick
And turns the gents to stone!

REACTIONS

Yawning is uncontrollable now
Missing pieces of my drive into work
Dizzy with lethargy, focusing is hard
Half my life in daily twilight sleep
Allergies make normalcy a pipe dream
So many dank drugs coursing through these veins
Sinuses are stuffed, unable to breathe
Without proper rest, reality fades
I'd keep my baldness if I had my way
Get rid of allergies and sleep, today

I'M NOT INTO YOU

I'm not into you the way people probably think I'm into you
I mean...
I can call a spade a spade
My blood is hot after all
But that's not how I dig you
Although I dig you
It's just that it wouldn't make you special
When everyone has a target on their back

I'm not into you the way people probably believe I'm into you
You've never been a childhood fantasy
Early on I might have though what if...
Who wouldn't?
But time changed fleeting feelings to familial
Now you and my siblings are on the same level
I'm not sure you're into me the same way I'm into you
And that's okay because this isn't adolescent pining
But you trust me with the big stuff
I'd like to think we enjoy each other's company

I'm not into what anyone thinks about what we have
Because what we don't have is pretense
We dropped that long ago
And that's not lip service
It's that I sincerely value your friendship
So the haters can hate
But I got you
And you got me
That's family

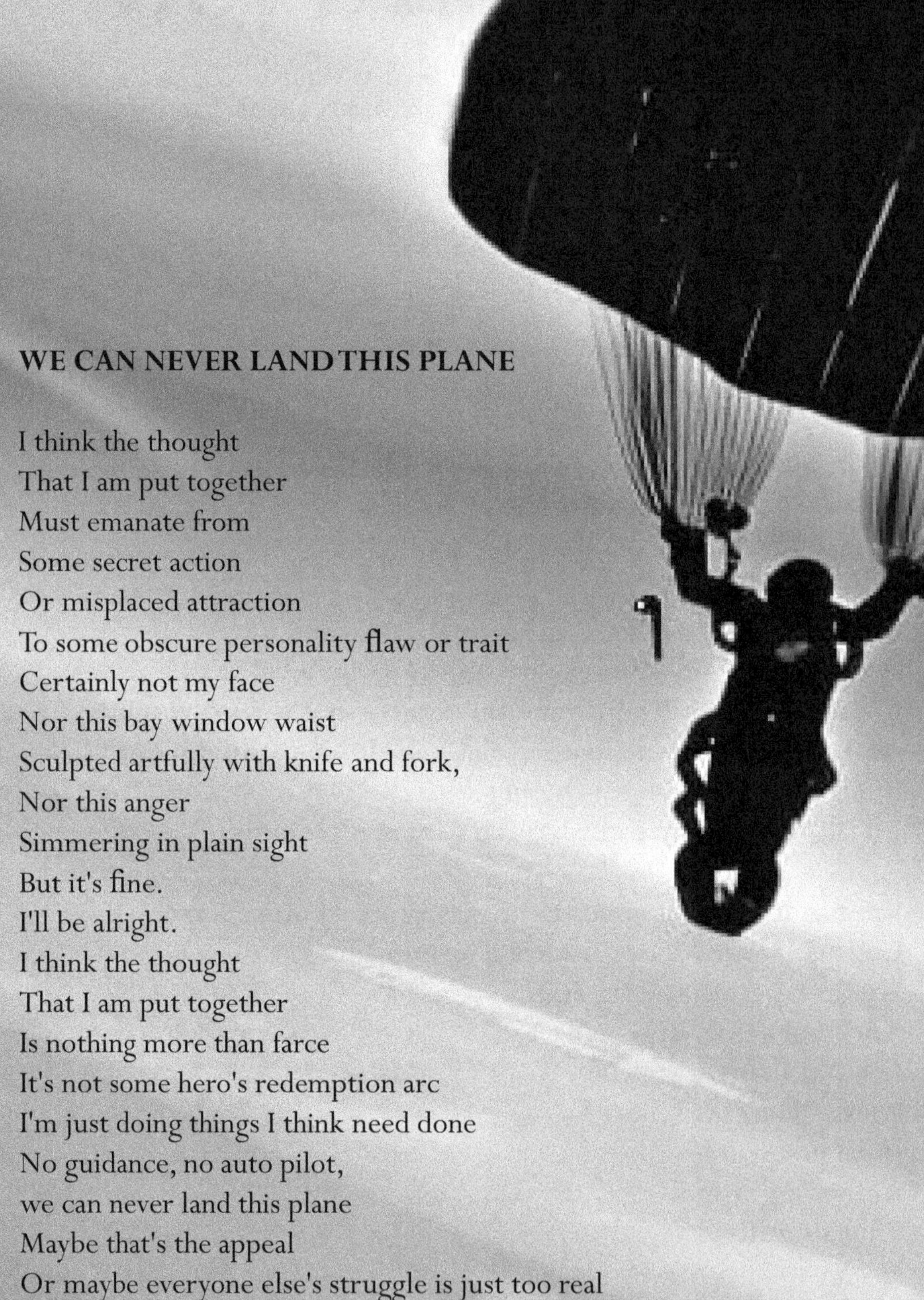

WE CAN NEVER LAND THIS PLANE

I think the thought
That I am put together
Must emanate from
Some secret action
Or misplaced attraction
To some obscure personality flaw or trait
Certainly not my face
Nor this bay window waist
Sculpted artfully with knife and fork,
Nor this anger
Simmering in plain sight
But it's fine.
I'll be alright.
I think the thought
That I am put together
Is nothing more than farce
It's not some hero's redemption arc
I'm just doing things I think need done
No guidance, no auto pilot,
we can never land this plane
Maybe that's the appeal
Or maybe everyone else's struggle is just too real
That a charlatan like me can pull enough wool over their eyes to make them
feel secure

PARLOR TRICKS

He only gives you what you can handle
A convenient lie told by people who have never had anything bad happen
To those poor souls they want to patronize
Can you imagine words so crass?
Spoken flippantly to the ghost of JonBenet?
What about when Never Bad Happens gives unsolicited feedback
To Jacob Blake shot in the back?
There are thousands of other snuffed souls every day
Every Karen on Facebook has something to say
A sharply spoken word smartly offered without request to Elizabeth Smart?
Six million godly anecdotes sweetly hissed in unison to the victims of the
second great war?
A more conceited play does not exist
A less invited piece of advice from the classist sexist dumbfuckists
A more improbable logical fallacy can't be found
The magic words to paint you an asshole.
But don't worry, he won't give you more than you can handle.

Pictured: God and Satan playing h.o.r.s.e. for the souls of man

A TREMENDOUS CALLING

From all directions it beckons
Sweetly calling for my company
Softly reaching for my hand
Assuring me it will not be that bad
A sales pitch for the great unknown
From every corner it calls my name
Softly urging me to act
Sweetly nudging me off track
Comforting me, who could resist?
This hard sell for permanent rest
But I'm not in any hurry.
I won't run to catch this train.
It will always be there if I need it,
A ray of light on my darkest day.

A BIRD AND A BIKE

Little bird
Perched on a stop light
Silhouetted against an auburn sky
Could you foresee that he would die?
Did you see the light turn green?
Did you see the car careen?
Could you so small prevent this mess?
Could you hear the cracks as chests compress?

    Little bird
    Perched on a stop light
    Herald of tragedy
    Were you aware in all the Earth
    That this is where the Reaper'd be?
    Could you see his sickle?
    Could you see his hood?
    Could you see the skid marks?
    From way up there?
    You should.

        Little bird
        Flying through an auburn sky
        Harbinger of tears
        You get to fly away
        Leave the bike behind
        Leave remorse in your wake
        But maybe you didn't know
        Maybe our need to move like you
        Is lost in you,
        The same way in two blinks
        We lose you in an auburn sky

SHAMEFUL WASTE OF TIME

This is going to sound conceited
But I should have found the cure
I should have cracked the code
I should have borne more weight
No need to share this load
I did not take advantage
I did not take the wheel
I left some in the hopper
I left some pages blank
I guess I should do better
I've only me to thank

THE TRAGEDY OF DARTH PLAGUEIS THE WISE

Well he dead so he's only half smart
The Senate determined to RIP the senate apart
Teaching young Ani things he shouldn't learn
And talking mad shit about the Jedis in Return
Did you ever hear it?
The tragedy that is?
Well that's the funny thing, cuz no one ever did
Sidious is cherry picking all the choicest deets
Weaving a clever tapestry of half-truths and deceits
Sure he sees the boy's potential, but there is also something more
A chance to use his power to destroy the Jedi order
Sheev gently pulls the levers
Whispering sweet words
The way he brings the acts together is borderline absurd
Preying on the simple, the fearful and the weary
The subtle moves are so nuanced it almost makes me cheery
A word in secret here, and a pseudo-statement there
And soon enough he'll bring unlimited power to bear
To watch the master pull the strings is surely a delight
See the darkness take its grip, choking out the light
Because the tragedy had naught to do with Hego Damask's sin
But everything to do with all the people taken in
You must always guard against promises too great
Or you and Ani Skywalker will share a common fate

THE TRAGEDY OF WHITE WOMAN AT STARBUCKS

If you listen carefully,
You can hear the call,
In every Target food court,
And nearly every mall.
A thousand tiny voices,
Calling out in vain,
"I think you ruined my order"
"That's not how you spell my name!"
There's no amount of yoga.
There's no prescription pill.
"I can't even with this right now"
There's just no way to deal.
Talk about entitlement!
No line that can't be cut.
"I'll just get a grande,
Lest it go straight to my butt"
Gallons after gallons
Of nature's wake-up brine,
Divvied out to Chads and Karens
From 6 to half past 9.
A dollar in the tip jar,
Then out the door she'll fly,
"If I don't get my coffee
I would simply die."
Addicted to this madness,
One sugar and two creams,
Constantly complaining,
The new American dream

THE TRAGEDY OF THANOS

Snap

It was inevitable

Of course they'd be avenged
But God Damn it
He's got a point

Snap

It was inevitable

He claims mercy
And I can't disagree
I do the same with radishes

Snap

It was inevitable

Nothing personal
But you don't quest this hard for this long
Unless it's personal

Snap

It was inevitable

Of course they'd be avenged
But culling the herd
Promotes growth

Snap

It was inevitable

He claims mercy
They missed a chance
To turn ashes into lemonade

Snap

It was inevitable

Nothing personal
But if the universe is left unchecked
It'll eat itself

Snap

It was inevitable

Of course they'd be avenged
But if not snaps
Then something else, more prolonged

Snap

It was inevitable

He claims mercy
He sacrificed his life
For his beliefs and his convictions

Snap

It was inevitable

Nothing personal
Though with so much at risk
How could it not be personal

Snap

It was inevitable

Of course they would be avenged
He claims mercy
Nothing personal

ARGUING WITH FRIENDS OVER POLITICS

I want to poke the bear
So I can really get into that skin
Encourage your biases to really set in
I want to extract what you really believe
Please, sear your policy into your sleeve
I know you say it's Adam and Eve and not Adam and Steve
But do you really believe or was it hammered into your head
You say you hate abortion but you'll let the mother end up dead?
You say you hate abortion but there are how many kids
Who can't afford tuition and don't know where their next meal is?
This isn't politics anymore
This is crumpling up morality and spiking it on the floor
You really think your god is gonna open heaven's door?
When you fuck a little kid for a few dollars more?
When you fuck a working mom for a few dollars more?
When you fuck a different color for a few dollars more?
You even fuck around on your wife with a whore
She's just hustling, trying to meet those ends
She'll suck a dick or two in the back of a Benz
Picking up the paper that you threw on the floor
She can cover rent with just a few dollars more
And she can cover food if she lets you in the back door
You put us all in this position
Just dogs, mauling for scraps
While you tell us all to work harder if we want out of this trap
So make your little laws
And redraw your little maps
Pull the little levers
Keep widening the gap
But also keep one thought in mind
While you're up there having fun
This club where you're a member
Thinks we all should own a gun

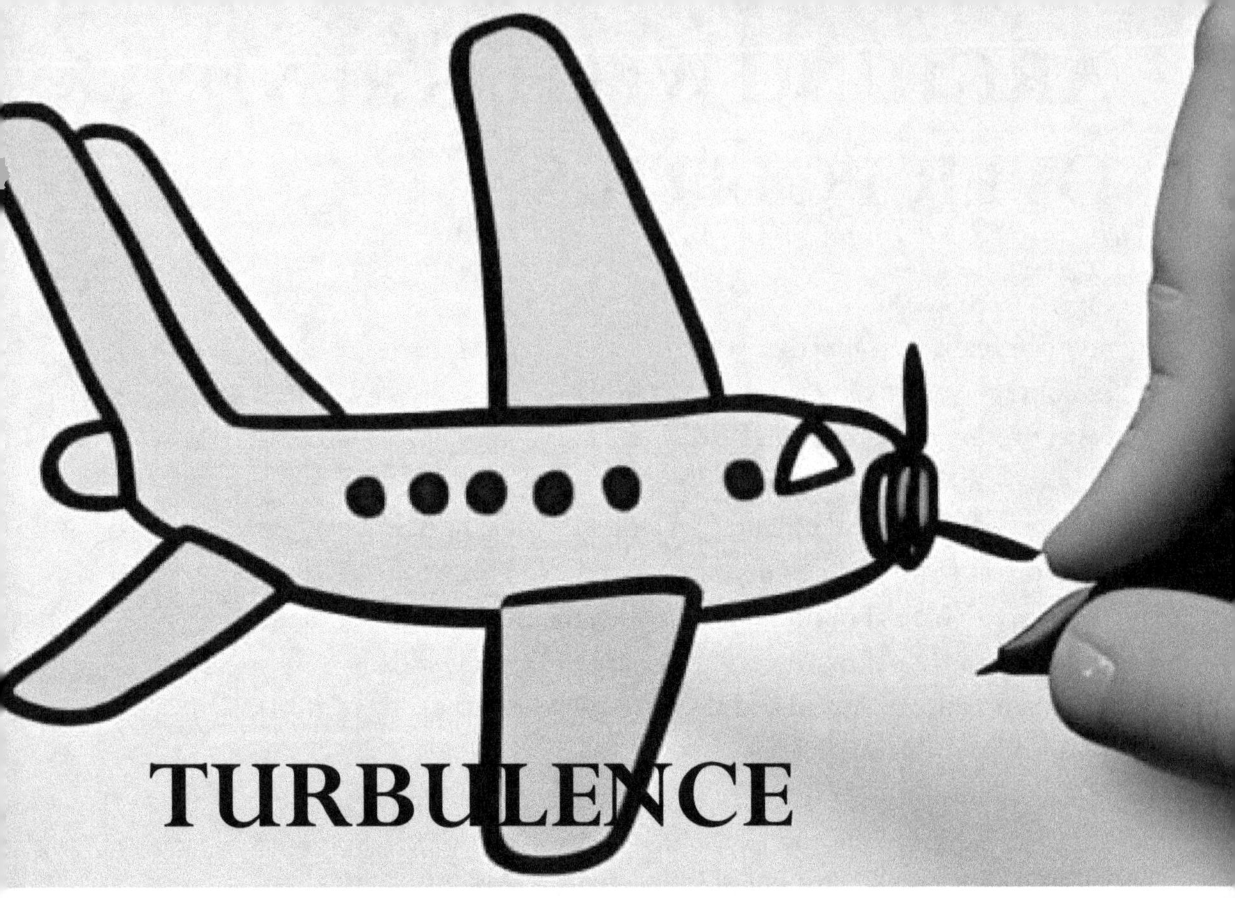

TURBULENCE

This airplane ride is like
Flying down a gravel road
Washboards bouncing after rain
From a careless county employee
Who scraped the rock into the ditch
Who couldn't keep a steady grade
We were traveling too fast in the White Trash Mobile
My '89 hand-me-down LeSabre

This flight is like a matchbox car
Maybe my General Lee
That I lost in the sandbox in 1992
Buried under sand that dad pulled out of the Nishnabotna River
And it's bouncing – like driving across a sushi roller
At the sushi counter
Of the Hy-Vee where we met

This airplane ride is like
A wooden roller coaster
At a small-town amusement park
Everyone rides it once
Then exhibits symptoms of a car crash
Like the time you took the corner toooo fast
And we almost both got whiplash
In your drab 1990 LeSabre
When there was brimstone in your voice
Because I turned up the radio
To better hear a song I liked more than you

This flight
May as well be at sea
With Brad Pitt or Chris Pine at the helm
At first everything was smooth
Almost too calm
But then on the horizon
I saw the storms building in your eyes
Like thunderheads on Kansas plains
Driving me to ground
Destroying the home I was trying to build
Howling as I scramble to hold on to anything

This turbulence made a great story
When I landed
I don't know if I was ever truly in danger
But I'm thankful that, unlike the LeSabres, I survived

THE TRAGEDY OF
GUY WITH TRUCK
NUTS ON HIS WHIP

Swing low, sweet pickup truck nuts
Tied to my hitch with number nine wire

Y'all see, reverse racist is a thing
Them beaners are gonna take all our jerbs

You ain't takin' my guns
A good guy with a gun is the only thing
Stoppen them Islams from shooting up are Wal-Mart

Crooked Hillary is a Deep State patsy
And probably a Nat-zee, and I know that dyke is a lesbian
No wonder Slick Willie was getting knobbers from that Monica

How come they don't investigate Benghazi
That Obummer wants Marshall law
He'll have it by Christmas, too.

It's corporations, man!
They want to keep us down
That's how they make money

And that socialist Bernie
Would take all my money and give everyone welfare
And he'd probably give it to them faggots too

Come and get it Bernie! Come and take my guns!

Trump just tells it like it is
He's a good businessman, and that Mueller is a secret agent for
the Demoncrats
He's trying to trick Trump

We need a wall. Them beaners are stealing our jobs and getting
free healthcare
Why should we help them? Why don't they fix their dumb
country?

All them feminists boycotting Trump
You know they just ask for it the way they dress
A woman's place is in the kitchen
And I don't like them hairy pits

Anyway, I can't prove none of this
I just know I'm right.
It's all corporations, man.
Do your research. You'll see.

THE TRAGEDY OF DEAD UNCLE JIM

The captain of this ship is Morgan
The only Daniel in this lion's den is Jack
When people needed to count on you
You never had their back

Always moving on
You'd talk about turning that new leaf
But New Years was still six months away
All your stints on the wagon were brief

The only thing you gave your loved ones
was heartache
You were getting strung along by someone
in my grade
You said you wanted to be something to
her
I asked, "A grandpa?" Then added, "Find
someone your own age."

Despite your flaws and failures
Your family stayed by your side
I even visited you in the hospital
It pained me to see your distended
stomach and yellowed hide

The day I got the phone call
I knew what words I'd hear
You couldn't change for loved ones
Too in love with whiskey and beer

But not all tragic endings
Fade out with cloudy skies
The lessons learned – what not to do
Still guide your nephew's life

When going through your belongings
I came across some poems
I promised I would read them
And so I took them home

The words made quite the impact
But not the way you think
Instead, a cautionary tale
That's kept me from the brink

I'd be a god damned fool
If I didn't come to grips
That blood that carried you away
Is the same blood that I drip

So this is what you left me
Two devils up my arms
A love for words and poetry
And a vow to never cause the same harm

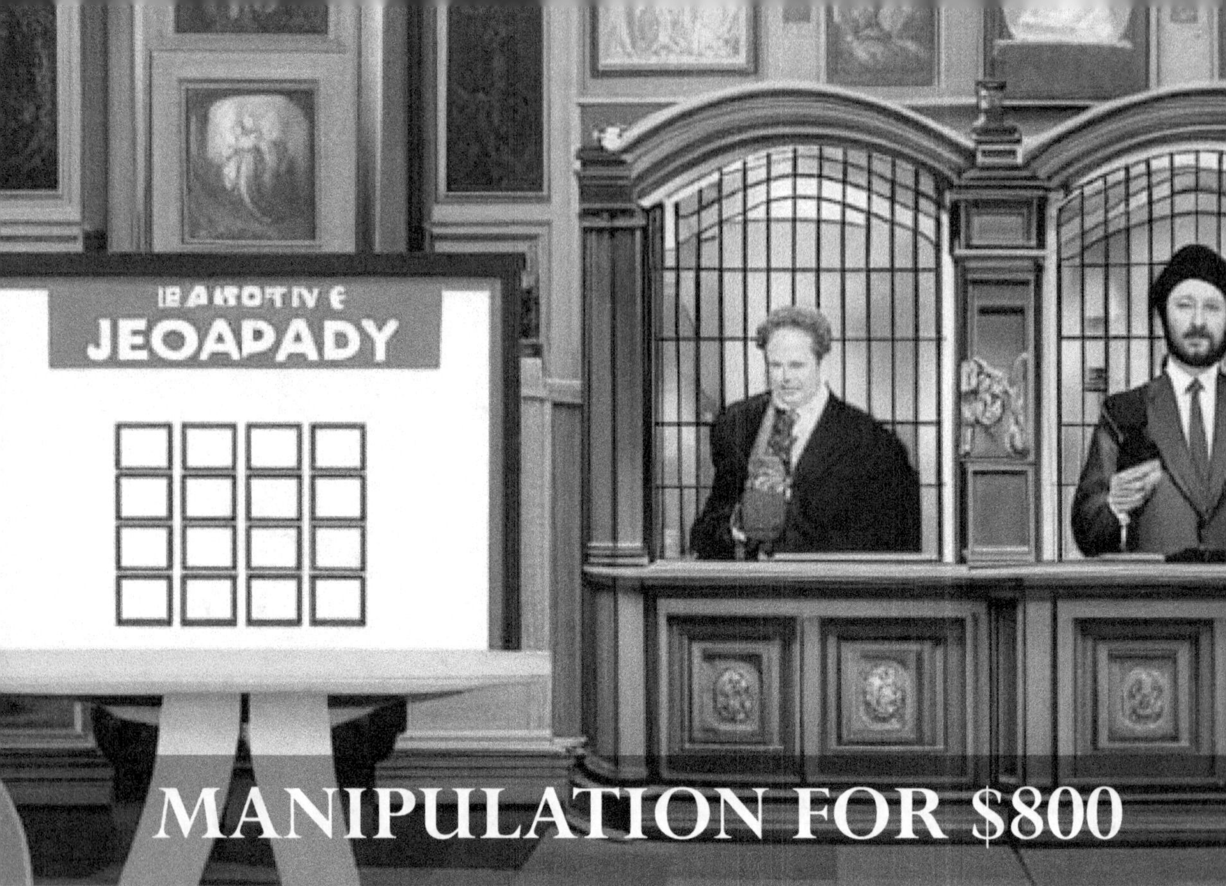

MANIPULATION FOR $800

The answer?
This relationship fizzled out without a clear ending.

The question:

Who is us?
What is apathy?
What is I still made the effort for two weeks when it was over in your mind?
What is hate?
What is fuel?
What is the worst part was not knowing what to do?
What is free time?
What is pain?
What is when we came back it was never really the same?
What is lucky?
What is I won?
What is when it was over was when I started to have fun?
What is the matrix?
Who is the one?
What is, it wasn't you and I'm so glad I dodged the bullets from this gun?

I'll take Happier Now for $2000 and make it a true daily double.

THE PARADOX OF CHOICE

Cookies.
Breads.
Soda pops.
Threads.
Pizza.
Eggs.
Pasta shapes.
Meds.
There are too many choices.
Everything looks the same.
How can something so trivial
Turn into something so lame?
I don't need 500 sauces.
I don't need thousands of jeans.
The longer it takes me to choose,
The less important it seems.
What you've mistaken as loyalty
Is inability to care.
I don't need 900 shampoo brands;
I don't even have any hair!
Stop trying to sell me variation!
Stop trying to get me off base!
How can anyone decide on location?!?
How can anyone pick a wash for your face!?!
All I need is some consistency......

The longer it takes to choose between two things,
the less it matters.

THE VINEGAR OF TIME

Time is a walking exit ramp at a professional team stadium
"I've been here before. This is exactly the same,"
You say at each level.
But that's not true.
Everything looks the same because you want it to.
To look the same.
To feel like you felt before.

But there are subtle differences the further you descend.
A concentric spiral stacked above and below.
Markings on the wall, vomit from a drunk,
Gum and worse imprinted on the concrete.
You want time to be a circle.
Life is a corkscrew opening poorly aged wine;
The vinegar of time.

ROI

Carol Burnett's show was everything true comedy
Aspires to be
Genuinely
Watch it today and you will see
The ROI on the show was gold
Jokes that age that well never get old

PINS

Kansas Bowling will probably never be my friend
But I think she's got an eye for my bullshit brand
How many of us are secretly in friend with someone else
But we let the ills of investment in others
Like time and effort
Slip away
Plus, how can you trust a stranger, when so many friendships fall asleep?

WHAT IT MEANS TO COPE

Upbeat words to describe an unhappy life
Despair turns to resignation, resignation turns to strife
It's such a dick move, to feel this way
But I'm perpetually angry, oh, you know, every day
It is so fantastic to feel so little hope
A perfect failure, a little piece of soap
Once you wash away your sins there's still a hanging rope
Is it fair?
Is it right?
I lie awake past the middle of the night
I can't forget, filled with spite
Stewing on the ways I've wasted life

THE GREAT LOTHARIO

He'll be ready to go at any time on the clock
I hope you've made your peace before you hear his knock
Death fucks with us all, the Great Lothario
Eternal cocksman, always ready for a go
Sometimes he likes it gentle
Most times he likes it rough
He's not afraid of an orgy
If everyone's time is up
Will you be his quickie?
Here one blink, gone the next?
Or will he woo you sweetly
Slowly doing what he does best?
Will his passion leave you breathless, and leave your corpse pristine?
Or will he dominate you and leave behind a scene?
No one knows for certain when they'll have their final tryst
That's why waiting till tomorrow is such an awful risk!
Tell the ones you love how you feel for them today
Once Death has his way with you there'll be nothing left to say!

STILLS

These memories aren't fleeting
They appear as stills
Still vivid
Playful under stars
Near the fountain I held your hand
All I did was talk, but you smiled anyway
Soon after
Pulling you close in stalks
Under moonlight sky
Lower lip bites
Feeling each other out
Washing my car on a Friday night
Two-hour drives felt hours longer
You took a job further from me
But I would drive twice as far on
principle
My tiny space
A trainer for reality
I called in late for work
So I could feel your skin radiate heat on
my lips
Another hours-long drive
Your mouth attacked me upon entry
My biggest regret
Setting your hunger aside to fill our
stomachs with granite

In your apartment
Our first time
You coyly seduced me with dexterity
Your nimble fingers like a piper's tune
Leading me higher and higher
After months of exploration
We summited
New York City beckoned
But that false idol paled in comparison to
your embrace
An embrace that was home regardless of
address
After, a long drive in snow ending in near
disaster
Another time I should have stayed with
you
Our biggest mistake
Glue that bound us through squalls and
even hurricane
The winds of turbulence couldn't unbrick
our foundation
That early excitement soaring still
As we write chapter after chapter
together

IN FLU

Social media
Social networking
Insta, pinsta, repeat after rinsta
How many fucking people can put "wandering" in their handle?
Maybe if you used Maps or Waze
You wouldn't wander for days
Maybe…
…I'm the one who's lost?
Trying to get famous on these superhighways
Hell, I'll break the fourth
You're only reading this poem because reasons
And those reasons are: Buy this book for money
Surely, honey,
No one wants to see me arch my back
To get that stack

SHORTY BOIS

Unless we make a leap
I'm on the downward slope
But some of his best years
Were late eighties era Bob Hope
Maybe getting old and dying
Is just part of the plot

Fuck your way to the top
Just like a Kardashian
There's no trick to it
It's just a simple trick

Nobody jerks off for pleasure
That's why I don't wear a smart watch
Matchbox 2020
It's three AM I must be jerking off to sleep
Cuz you know I'm not running a midnight 400
Just to get a jump start on my steps

If Clive Owen's mustache
Fought Tom Selleck's
Who would win?
Me.
Maybe you, too.
I don't know what revs you

Kevin Costner
A rich man's Uncle Jim,
I lived vicariously through Robin and Frank
Later,
Uncle Jim died.
I won't wait until New Year's to turn over a new leaf

What if Ted Danson
Was made out of
Tiny Tony Danzas
Like Optimus Prime
He'd be the fucking boss

James Dean
Million dollar peen
Lindsay Lohan
Flash in the pan
I'd pay eight bucks today
To see Freaky Deeky Friday

THE CRAFT

Chuck and Neil aren't better than me
They are simply more dedicated
They are to writing as a craft
As I am to tomfuckery

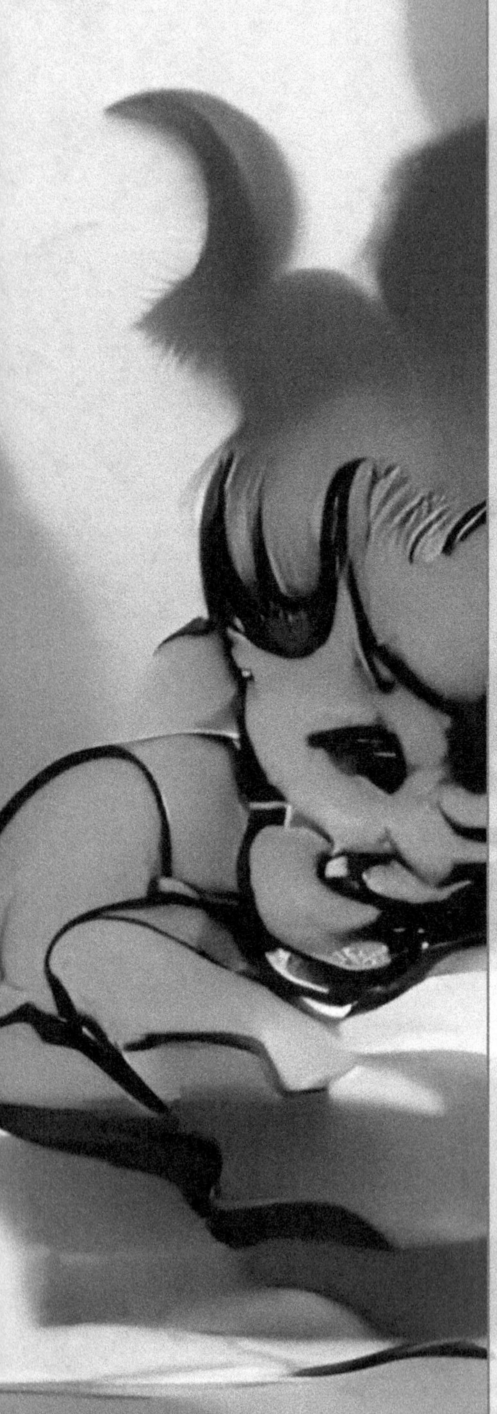

YOU LIE

I know the way you lie
I can see it in your looks
I read you like my favorite book
I know the way you turn a phrase
You're set in your old ways
Like a verse on my favorite page
Like how anything goes with beige
You'll tie this room up in a knot
This kind of power can't be bought
They say the truth will save
But I'd rather be a slave to you
You keep me young
Just like a fountain,
these magic words are flowing from your tongue and
You keep me high
Even when I'm in the dumps
You know the truth would leave us stumped
Yes, I know the way you like to lie

I know the way you lie
There's a devil in your grin
And a smile in your eye
I see how you cut and run
These words are bullets in your gun
The truth is not as fun
If I'm gonna make it through
I'll need the best of you
And the best of you is always make believe
I hold you in my heart and wear it in my sleeve
You keep me young
Just like a fountain,
these magic words are flowing from your tongue and
You keep me high
Even when I take my lumps
You know the truth would leave us stumped
Yes, I know the way you like to lie

PRISON SENTENCE

DO THE CARPETS MATCH THE CEILING?

Marijuana Woman, Motel 6 Man
We get together every time we can
Stupid old kids and job can't keep us apart
There's too much love in this nooner's heart
Pay by the ¼ hour is a real good start

See that pig waiting nearby
But we're horny as shit and sporting red eyes
When the pig gives us a long hard up and down
We ditch the Motel 6 and head downtown
Find a Red Roof Inn and we'll go to town
Paint the ceiling white and the carpet brown
Trash the room then it's peel out sounds
So long suckers, see you around
You can't catch us, pig, because we don't slow down

HARD ARNIE

When life gives you lemons
Take a giant bite while staring back
Few can manage the sour burst
Suck in your breath and make it worse
There's nothing you can change
Embrace the pain like you're deranged
No one can hurt you if you like the way it feels

IN DEFENSE OF BEATING UP KIDS

What's at stake here is consequences
These little pricks think they can get away with everything
But they forgot I can serve a sentence
They forgot I know how to win a war of attrition
(Just die the most)
So when your little kid kicks my shin
Rest assured I'm kicking back
And if your kid taps my sack
You've never heard a belt make such a crack
What's at stake here is consequences
Actions have them
And learning a hard lesson early is easier than later
Plus, kids heal fast

A READER'S RESPONSE TO LIFE

Everyone's responses are valid
Education breeds acknowledgment
A derelict's elation over a poem about flowers
Is no less relevant than a Pope's
Never mind the loss of metaphor on a green or addled brain
Even the Pope has prejudice and preconception

We're all an evolving sculpture
Like majestic peaks wearing and worn over time
If experience is the artist, sculpting and molding
It's hard to discount any art as long as it doesn't show regression
And even regression can be growth
Even pain and even lack of education

Raw pieces of granite have limitless potential in the hands of the right artist
People are a victim or conqueror of their circumstance
Even the Venus de Milo is missing her arms
Everyone's got their damage, but everyone's got their hopes
So how can a derelict's elation over a poem about flowers
Be any less relevant than a Pope's?

UNIMPORTANT LONGNESS

pretty face
bad taste
long legs
blue eggs
big tits
pop flies aren't hits
killer body
i have to go potty
flowing hair
polar bear
pretty eyes
helpless cries
small feet
baseball cleat
dainty hands
marching bands
long nails
five gallon pails
white skin
roofing tin
furtive glance
nice pants
crazy thought
goodness gracious she's hot

ACID REFLUX

Are you real
Are you a dream
I always
Want to find you
But in a fog it seems
You disappear
I wonder
If I'll find you
I always have this fear
That everything I'm looking for
Is on the other side
Of a giant mirror
And if I break it
It's gone
But if I let it go
It just stares at me

I LIKE DOLPHINS

I like dolphins

    Caught in whale nets

Cause they are pretty

    No they aren't

I like Thompson's Gazelles

    When cheetahs eat them

Cause they run fast

    And bleed a lot

I like my roommate

    He does drugs

He is good at math

    He is good at staring into oblivion when he is stoned

I liked my dog

    He was dumb

My neighbor shot him

    Crazy fuck

When did Father Time die

    Mom's knickknack drawer smells good

When did nature run its course

    Elvis wore a top hat

Green is everywhere

    The toilet backed up

I enjoy marshmallows

    I have shit on my floor

Candy is yummy

    My house smells like human shit

The French have good perfume

    Call the Mario Bros.

Ronald MacDonald

    There is a pube in my sandwich

Do you have a punch card?

    I didn't make my sandwich

Nomad

Candle

Campus
crack
pen 15 Club
Where is the border?

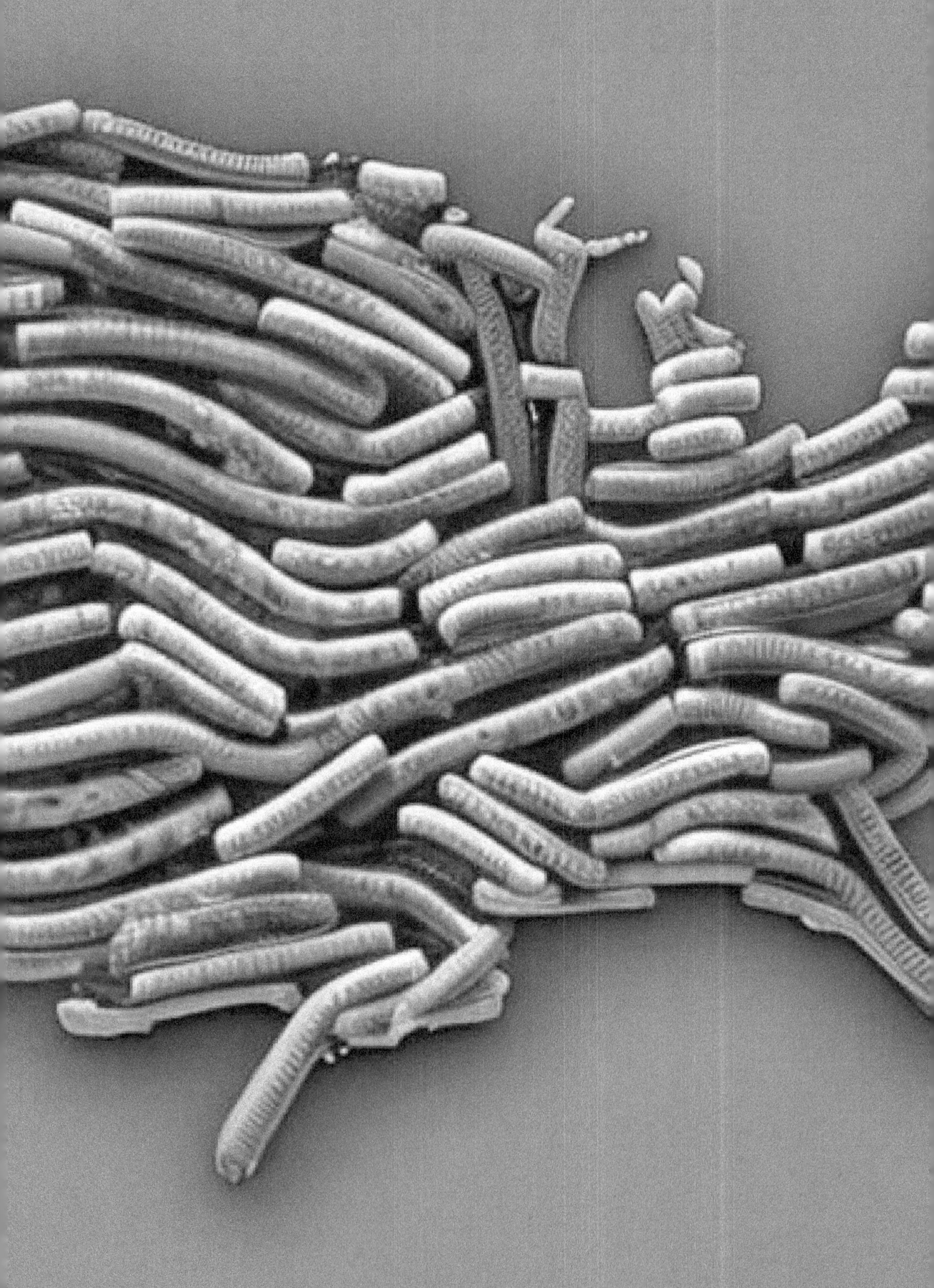

JIMMY DEAN'S SAUSAGE PARTY

Jimmy Dean
Didn't make it across America
But his sausage did
I like wrenches because they allow more torque
I don't like Mindy but I especially hate Mork
I wanted to say
That I liked your hair
But your crossed eyes distracted me
Why do you cross your eyes and not your legs?
If you did the additive inverse of sex
I could be your first
Tiddly winks

                                    Rapist
Why does your dad like
                                    Sodomy
How do you feel about
                                    Economy
When every one of your vessels has returned to shore
and mom has supper ready

Can you look your brother in the eye?
Knowing you slept with his girlfriend?

BETELGEUSE

When Betelgeuse goes supernova I hope I am alive to see. Looking up at Orion's Shoulder to witness an exploder. Scientists proclaim that it will cast earthly shadows at night, appearing with the strength of a half moon shining bright. Experts believe that human beings will see it in daylight. Adding that Earth is not at risk from the expanding radioactive disk. Residents of our planet will have ample warning thanks to particles setting off local electromagnets. All of civilization will have an unobstructed vision to cataclysm. Noises from the crowd will range from oohs and ahhs, with some laughing and the worst of us offering applause. Personally, I'll spend my time ruminating on whether the local aliens were successful evacuating. Imagine, knowing the time was set for your planet's imminent death. A blast so fierce and decisive that nothing will live. Do you think they got away in a pod? Do you think they still believe in God? Our most faithful will certainly not hesitate answering. "It was God's plan that the star would end." They will promote his celestial feat without any tongue in cheek. Gleefully reveling in this star's finale, unaware that their own leveling is also in the works. We don't know the date, but we certainly can expect a shared fate. No doubt witnessed by a distant society, who will point and laugh while championing their own deity. An endless loop of misplaced faith; the universe's long con, cosmic egg on their face.

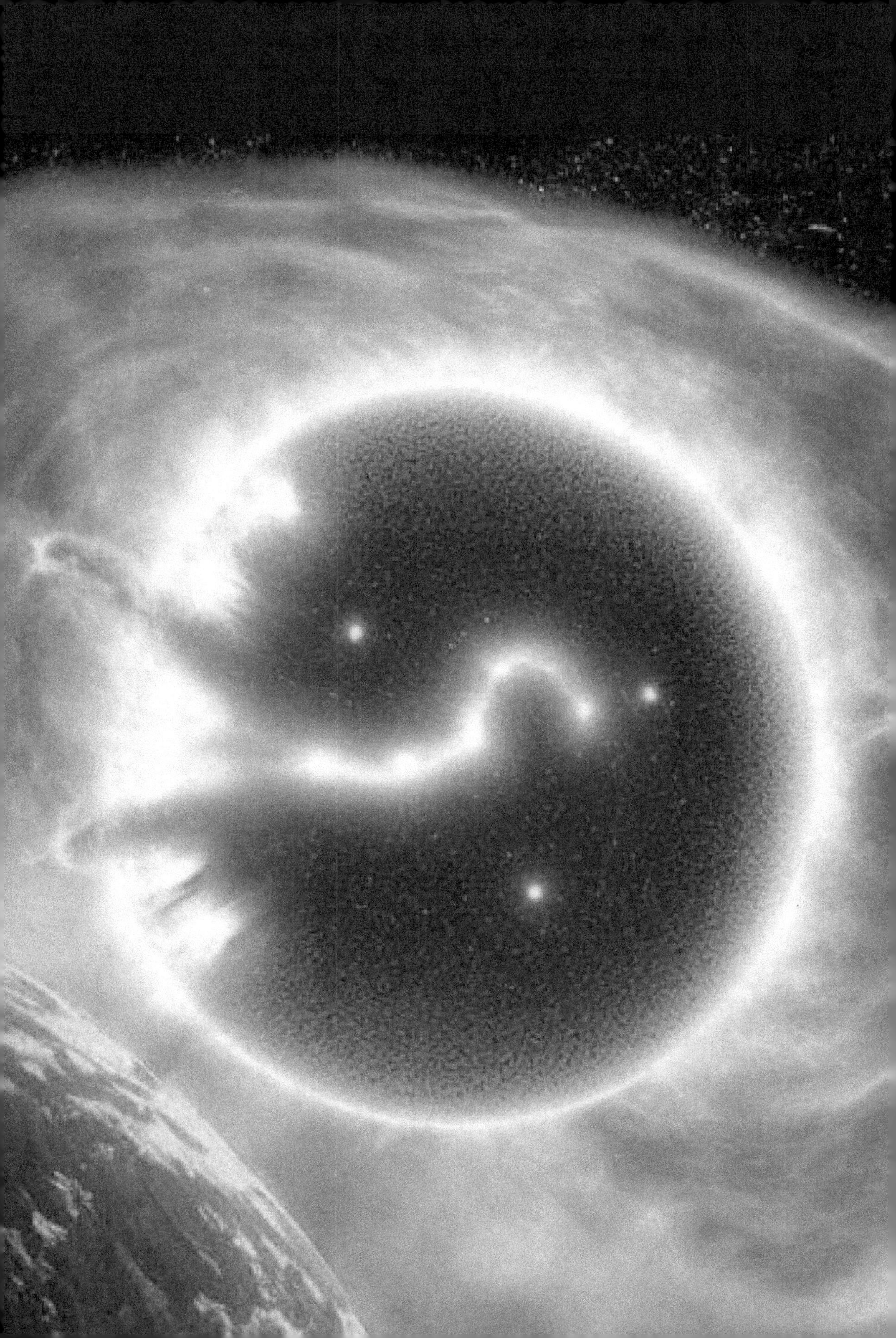

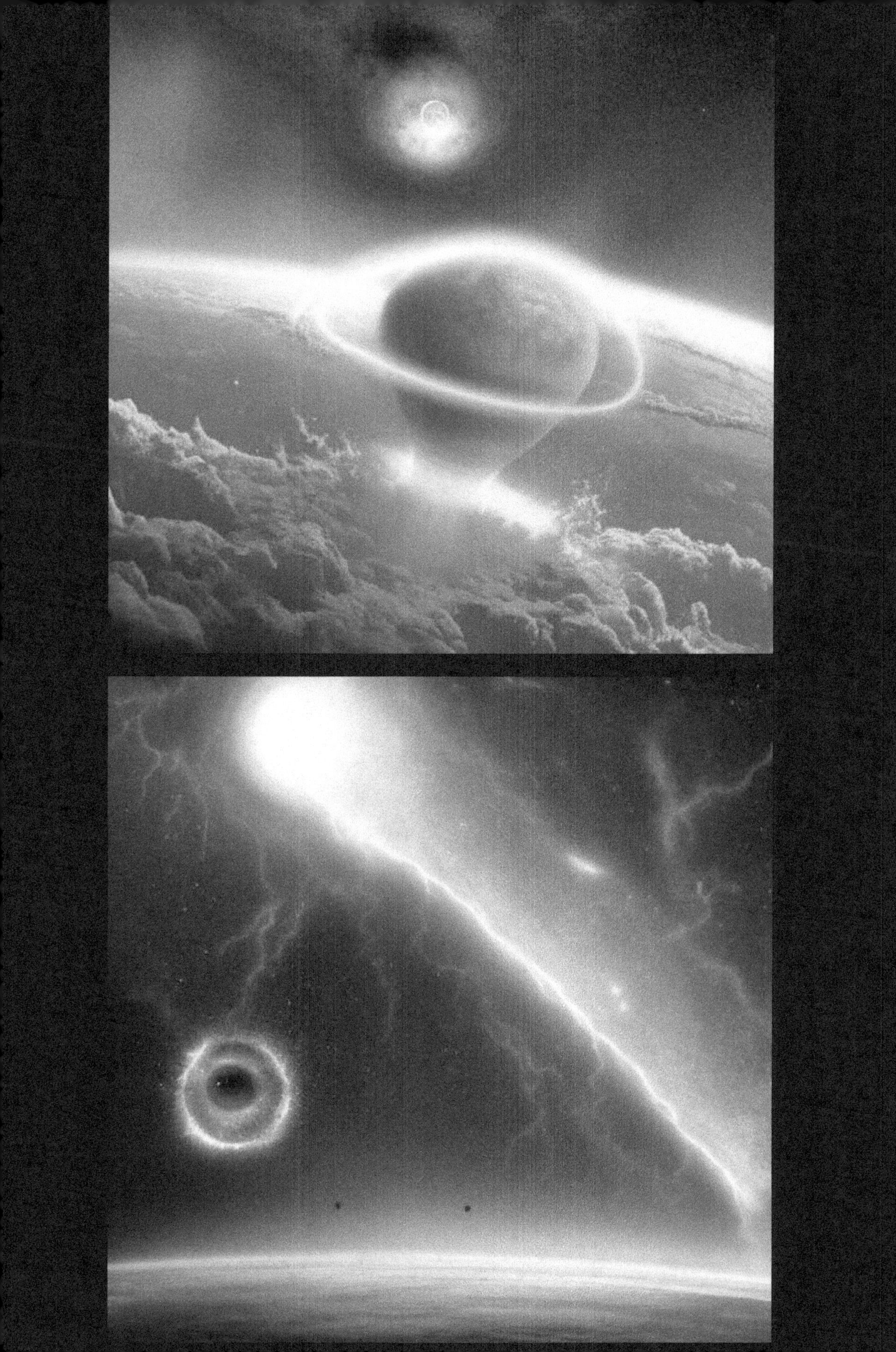

HEATWAVE

Hot and sweat
No breeze
To rage stiff against trees
Boiled air
Belligerent sun
A small passing cloud
Makes it feel like we've won

ME AND YOU AND ALL YOUR FAMILY AND EVERYONE YOU EVER KNEW OR CARED ABOUT

Everyone is a butthole
Me as well as you
We just gleefully sprinkle our bullshit
An endless number two
None of it really matters
All of it is certainly fake
We create our bullshit worlds
Then die once it's made
I just find it side splitting
When we draw our last number
Someone else can take over the shitting
What a god damned bummer
For the ones who carry on
But it doesn't really matter
Because they will also soon be gone
Just more useless footnotes
Little diamonds on this manure ring
The sooner you figure this out
The fewer days you'll waste time rueing

LOOSE TEETH

If I were a woman right now
I WOULD BE SO FUCKING MAD!
The least of all being the Olympic committee
Deciding larger swim caps are banned
Not to mention how they planned to punish new moms
Yet civility prevailed as mothers handled it with aplomb
As we climb the stairs of horseshittery
Women watched courts keep shackles on Britney
Siding with a drunken abuser
In lieu of believing the accuser
Courts and judges who side with abusers lined up far to near
Yet not one act of violence from gun nor knife nor Spears
And then the shit flavored icing on the bitter pill
The untimely release of noted rapist Cosby, Bill
I mean, what the fuck are we doing? What have we become?
How do these misogynists keep getting elected despite being so dumb?
I am a white man from Iowa who can skate right through life
And this shit makes me so fucking angry I can't sleep at night
The way this country treats women and minorities is past cause for alarm
The way it churns them out through various harms
I think it's due time for some to take a back seat
Choose their next actions carefully while they still have their teeth
And I know you might say that violence isn't a good plan
But maybe it's time to speak in a god damn language they'll understand

AUTHOR NOTE: Imagine my surprise (or complete lack thereof) two years later when they overturn
Roe v. Wade and also DeSantis is trying to go after trans folks the same way Hitler went after Jews.

SOUL EUCHRE

The yellow devils
Down the street
We play euchre
With their souls

I'M NOT A NICE MAN

I'm not a nice man
I don't do nice things
I dream about your sister playing on a sex swing
When I say hi to your mother
There's a double meaning
When I finish with the movie
I'll invite you to the screening
What a handsome pelt
Have you not heard of preening?
It's life lessons I am giving
Is it knowledge you are gleaning?
Or are you taking offense?
The way you took on love from other gents?
I am a product of your inventions
Whether or not it was your intention
To put me out to pasture?!
I know I'm an asshole but I wasn't a bastard
Until you dashed upon the stone
The one small thing I could call my own
You picked away pieces of me
Like the way crows feed on a rotting beef
I don't want to talk to you
Don't want to hold your hand
No matter how many times you call to apologize
I'm not a nice man

PROPANE CHILI

You win some you lose some
You bitch slapped your boozed mum
Your sister isn't married
All advances have been parried
Can't you smell what I am spelling?
Can't you feel me when I'm yelling?
Has your daddy flew the coop?
Did you brain him with a scoop?
Did your uncle part your waves?
Does your aunt deny the lays?
All your cousins are indicted
Their friends and friends' friends are spited
So gather 'round the sitting log
While dad and uncle roast the birthday hog
It will not take a CSI
To discover why your grandma cries
Every time she sees your face
Every time they bring up race
One time at your neighbor's place
He force-showed you how a gentleman tastes
A clearing house of information
A textbook case of degradation
While he placed his elimination
On your youthful mask of expectation
Can you rhyme a word with whoring?
Yes I can – it's old and boring
I get life dealt you a shitty hand
But you've done nothing to leap from pan
You'd probably just end up back in fire
A lit dumpster, out for hire
Blaming woes on passerbyers
Sympathy fades for constant criers
Words, a weapon you can't wield
Behold, the fucks I've sown in this field
An empty harvest like your skull
Your addled thoughts add up to NULL

MILEY CYRUS AIN'T GOT SHIT ON THIS WRECKING BALL

I threw the controller and in one swift motion became a wave of unbiased destruction.

The dinnerware shattered into a million pieces of emotion as I brought an Eastwing claw hammer down on it with the force of a 21-cannon salute; sending chunks of bowl flying into space at angles defying the theories of general relativity.

Turning, I focused all of my aggression on the Subway steak sandwich sitting on the ottoman.

The Subway steak sandwich had never hurt me, and my friend was probably excited to enjoy this sandwich, but I hurt the sandwich, and I hurt it well and hard, and when I was done, it was reduced to a wreck of torn emotion and violent destruction, just the ghost of a sandwich, maintaining the fetal position and sucking its thumb.

I dipped my hand in crime scene, which flowed like horror gore from open wounds.

"That's a good sandwich," I said, and walked out, leaving the now lifeless meal and distraught friend grasping for answers.

MAX vs. DAD

Again something happened
I did not know how
I was only doing what you asked
But on my watch things turn out poorly

Again something happened
I did not know how
I was only trying to think ahead
But anticipation is not my forte, you said

Again something happened
I did not know how
I was only doing the chores like you wanted them
But still I fell short of the goal

Again something happened
I did not know how
You were expecting were beyond what I could deliver
I disappointed you

Again something happened
I did not know how
We could not convey our differences
In an adult type setting

Again something happened
I think that I know how
We can fix the problem
And salvage this savagery

Again something happened
This time I know how
We have a strong relationship
And we talked it over and worked it out

Lisa Left Eye Lopez
People stop your mourning
Over her
I'm sorry she is dead
But for real
I don't care
Because anyone who has nine in the whip
Deserves to wreck

They deserve what they get

THE GOLDEN RULE

If you eat
Money sandwiches
Golden grapes
Or succulent silver sausages
You still could not buy my heart
With your shit

I WISH I COULD GIVE MY SKELETON A SHAKE

Crash my car deep down in ditch
So my limbs fly every way which
May cause something worse that I wish to avoid
In lieu of that I could toss myself into the void
Bouncing down the rock wall to rattle my bones
Every bump pumping out those rich tones
Unlikely I'd reassemble how I wish
I could try laying in gravel, then flopping like a fish
Maybe I could remove my spine and crack it like a whip
Then run sideways into a spike to loosen this hip
Fall flat on my back flying out of a tree
Land so hard all the wind is stolen from me
Rush headfirst into a falling down the stairs spree
Beg Masvidal for a flying knee
Deliver it with a kiss just under left shoulder
Make it feel like I've been hit by a boulder
Knock me backwards through space and time to my crib
Whatever it takes to reposition this rib
I can see it now: "Did it hurt?" you'll say
"Anything to align this vertebrae…"

TO NOT SINK

Today was just a fog
Rolling in through twilight sleep
Hanging over the harbor
Shrouding all the ships
And no matter how much coffee I drank
I could not give it the slip
I kept the crew below deck
Tried to limit how hard I had to think
Some days it is okay not to set sail
It's enough to just not sink

A FINE BLEMISH

The dots
Are what struck
And then they were bigger splotches
And then the little faces
And now the types of clothes
Finally, the whole
And I was not completed
Like the work
Because I was a work myself
I am a work myself
I am unfinished text
I am

HAIKUS

It is not much yet
It is honest work, you know
This, the game of memes

The moment she drops
The booty and the whole place
Goes fucking bonkers

Beyonce put a
Ring on it of platinum
Some declare her queen

Whence Kev spilled chili
Ten years later to the day
A good meme was born

Lest I say it twice
Stop all the pussy grabbing
You mother fucker

Only took four snaps
In the end, a Stark contrast
Still, most things set right

I am the senate
A surprise to be sure, not
An unwelcome one

In a galaxy
Far far far far far away
Midichlorians

Jar Jar Binks, secret
Sith, the only ones who deal
Among absolutes

Ben, a metaphor
Of religion, misguided
Feelings cloud the truth

Doin' a butt chug
Ain't worth denying, I say
It's only justice

Touching the queen E
The classless tactless orange
Walls off her support

How's it almost Ten?
My time just disappears these
Days. What a bummer.

We sit in our rooms
Waiting to exonerate

Waiting to appropriate

Or conjugate our liquid Draino lives

And then we meet in the fields
And we all are riding on wheels
But we didn't make them
We stole them
We punched holes in them
We ran around the circus tent and offered up our souls to them
And then they took us out to lunch

And it hurt a bunch

Sometime between the liquid state of our lives
And then they didn't pay for much
Others decided to shun

Was it a pun?
Was it a gun?
Was it fun?
When it was done?

Exclamation point
Is where we are
Models are
Our superstars
Not women
But models
Made of clay
An idol we call Mary Kay
High maintenance peanut butter faces
A mighty mix of seven different races
Rising in masses to show us our places
And all the while we smile
We see it not for what it is
A couple of bullets
A couple of kids
A couple of smiles
A couple of nods
High priced gas
And a denial of God
And a shadow disperses
And a monkey learns math
And tyrant shows mercy
Now I own a giraffe

Then the styles come back into style
So we wear pants that are basically recycled
And we the visage
The proud and commissioned
Show the lessers what it is like
Dream of the good things
Dream of the life
Work all your years
Give it your all
Just keep on trying
Who cares if you fall?
Give them the fish
But teach them not
It's not our job
To babysit the lot
Make the most of your talents
But without dirty hands

In a world of runarounds
Who
Wears
The
Pants

THE FLOWERS ARE STILL STANDING

After a year of resentment
Of having things both material and immaterial
Yoinked like tablecloth from under place setting
Today was the first day where I felt like
The flowers were still standing

6 DEGREES OF COOKING BACON

If Kevin Bacon came to town, the first thing he would see
Would be
The people of different races
And hopefully he wouldn't care so much that they were not all white
It is all right
If they are different
But the part that gets me about this town, and the part that would
Get Kevin
Is the smell
Not just the smell of factories and cars and dead animals and packing plants
But of diversity
And prejudice
Because in this town there is an undercurrent of harsh feelings not just
With the whites
Or with the Mexicans
Or with the Laos folks or the Chinese or the African American people
Mr. Bacon would
See a town
Where arguments and controversy run deep but where no one wants to do
Anything at all
About anything at all
Yes, Kevin would see a place where babies are disposed of in the literal sense
And cops are dicks
And the bars are meat markets
Smelling almost worse than the sweet and sour shit smell emanating from IBP
On the south side
And the east side
Of the plant located right next to a meat market of human flesh where Mr. Bacon
Could pick up
A local girl
And whether or not she was clean as the air that turns the windmills or as dirty
As the water
In the lake
It would not matter because pussy is pussy to Kevin Bacon and in this town
The only thing that tastes
Worse than local pussy
Is the KFC near the IBP, which kills meat next to the meat market
Where they deal
In human flesh
Which is by the lake that's by the road that leads to the college which is the only reason
Mr. Kevin Bacon
Would ever come
To this god-forsaken shit hole that I so fondly refer to as home

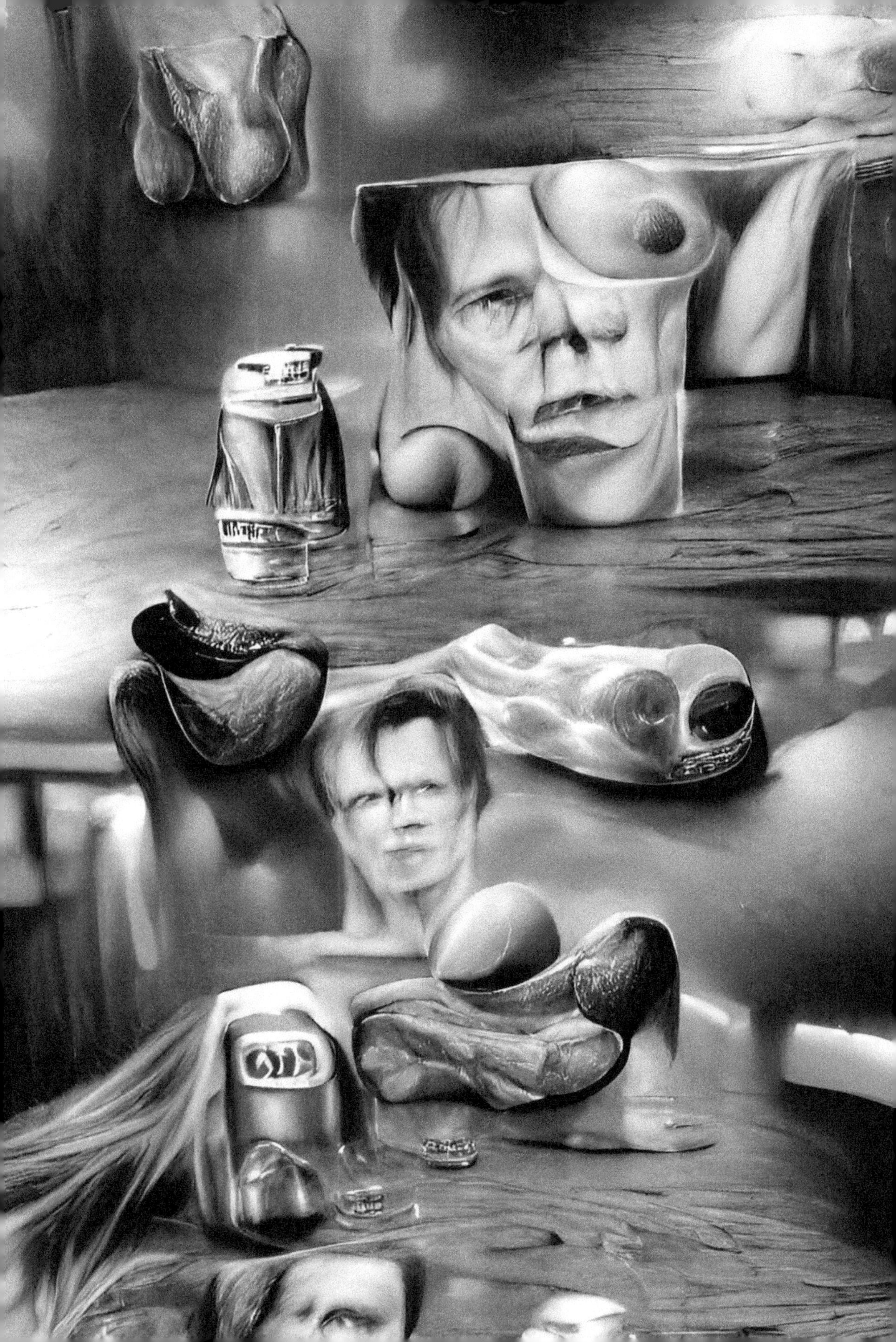

"HEY ROCK. TAKE HER TO THE ZOO. I HEAR RETARDS LIKE THE ZOO."

A rhino at the zoo
Runs to the fence
The children are scared

The elephant stands
The boy notices
A fifth leg

Mother yells at Billy
He wants a hot dog
An ostrich eats fruit

Sharks swim overhead
A diver scrubs the tank
With a special brush

Seals bark loudly
The alligators hear them
And become hungry

The ticket taker refunds money
The patrons walk
Lions growl

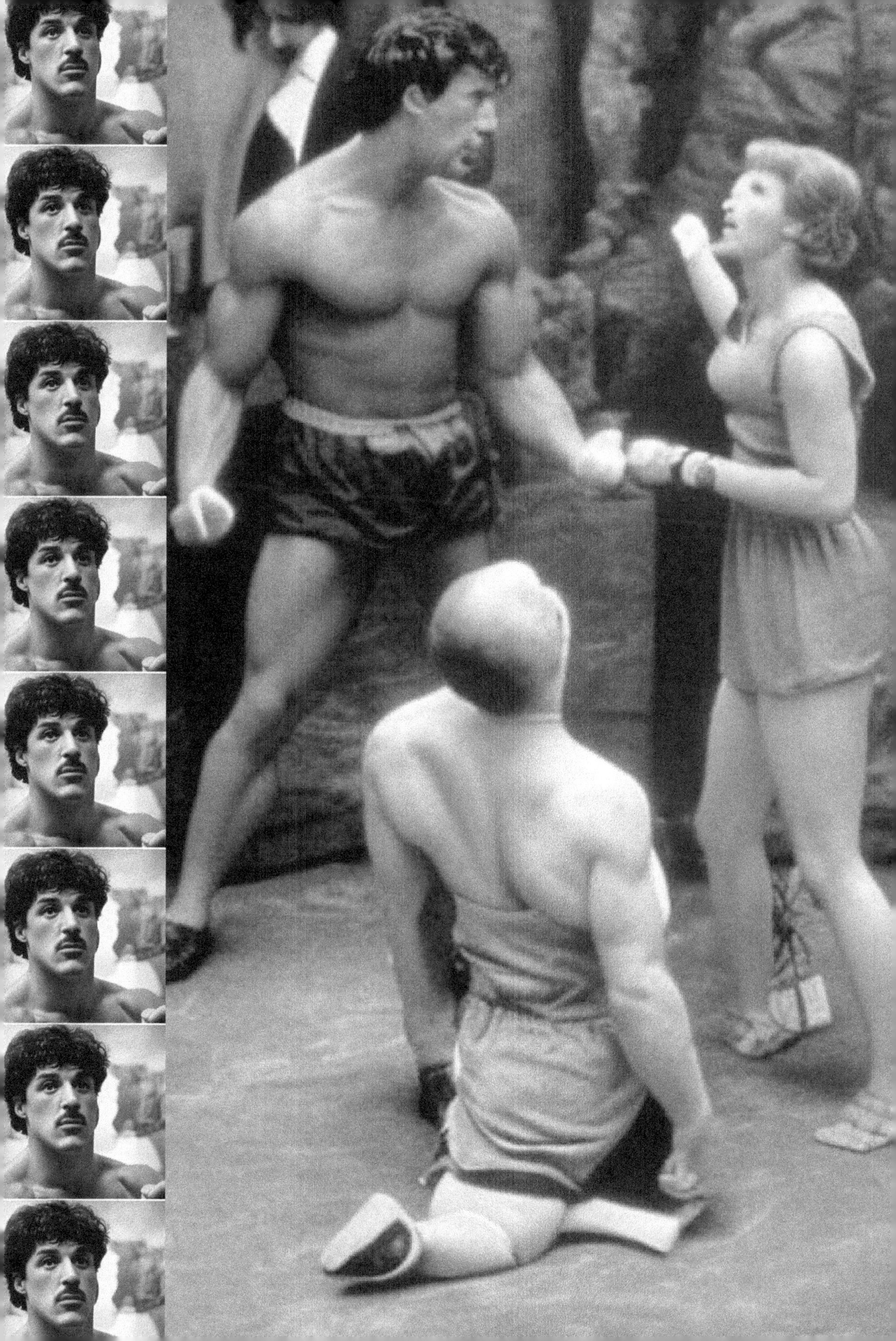

BOYO

The boyo
Speaks to the wonderful women out there
Saying things like
"Hey baby
"Hey bitch
"Hey woman"
He shows off
By playing Frisbee
With his slicked lips from
The delicious strawberry all-natural balm
But tonight
Like every night
Boyo will not be with the wonderful women
He will be at home
In his sock
But it makes for easier clean up
Than the tiger of birth, ready to pounce

A PLANT OF FACES

The Royals were back in town
We were going
Right after church
Right after God
So happy.
I ran from the church
Attempted to jump the railing
Near the north side door
Not knowing or forgetting
The other side
Had downward steps
I caught my foot
And I fell.
There were only two witnesses
My good friend Greg
And a man named
Wesley Walker
Who Greg's dad calls Eastly Runner
But before Wes could get to me
To check for a pulse
I was up cradling my face like a boy
Cradles his dog
When recently struck by a truck
The boy cradles his dying dog
The milk man stops to say he is sorry
Father checks on him to see if he is alright
I had the cradle,
I apologized to myself,
But God never came to make sure I was alright
Or maybe the fact
I felt embarrassed
Was his way of saying
At least you still feel.

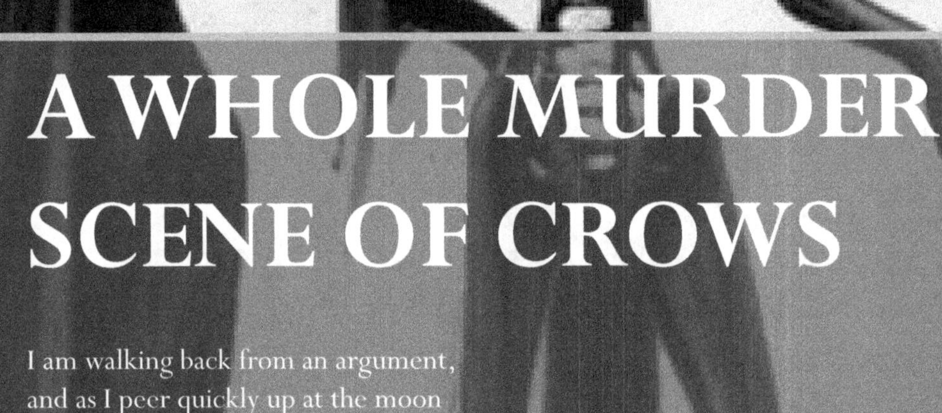

A WHOLE MURDER SCENE OF CROWS

I am walking back from an argument,
and as I peer quickly up at the moon
I note the fog forming a veil. I meant
to look for the dish and look for the spoon.

There are crows flying through the veil tonight.
Do they look identical to the moon?
Do they e'er enjoy the veil in mid-flight?
Are they afraid of getting hit by spoons?

Moving quickly away from the veil we,
as in myself and I - the crows and moon -
we leave quickly to escape this with glee,
ducking and dodging the dish and the spoon

We stop the fighting and nursery rhymes,
our life is a riddle most all the time

I LOVE THE SMELL OF RELATIVITY IN THE MORNING

I washed my car
My windshield was white and brown
The snow falls
Covering all of the landmarks
I don't know how to be a cartographer

If the Milky Way and Andromeda merge
I think I would stop
All traces of me would freeze
What kind of a name is Milky Way?
I lived my life in just one day

Where I am standing I feel alone
Events and memories rush by me in a blur
Yet when I throw a rock there is an arc in its path
Am I the one moving?
Is it me going fast and the world going slow?

I am running at the speed of light
I die and am born in the same instant
It's hard to progress in a world
Where everything is offsetting
Do you know how much life sucks when you're perfectly content?

Upstairs a woman screams
Without investigating she is both dead and alive
She is both raped and loved
She is both there and not there
Do you ever wonder why some things feel repeated?

I used to feel bad for the people who make mistakes
Some people are just evil
If they repeat the same mistakes for eternity
They always hurt the same people
Without an end, where is the retribution?

Daily I travel through time
With my memories and imagination
I went golfing with Greg once
He knew everything I was going to say
I wonder, did he remember or foresee?

ESCAPE OR EXPLODE

The ship was leaving that evening, a final endeavor to permanently sever from a dying planet. As people made their way to board it became clear they had miscounted bodies and feet. Outlook for departure became bleak for those without a guaranteed seat. Unrest became disquiet, disquiet became a riot. The crowd began to turn on each other, mom vs. mom, sister vs. brother. As fear turned to pain among the molten lava that began to rain, a giant chunk ripped the shuttle in twain, cascading debris and hopes to swirl down the drain. Now no one was getting off of this rock, everyone was stuck, their fates now locked. Imminent hopelessness washing in waves. The just and pitiful took to their knees while the depraved began their final raid. The last mass extinction playing out before our very eyes.

I think about this all the time.

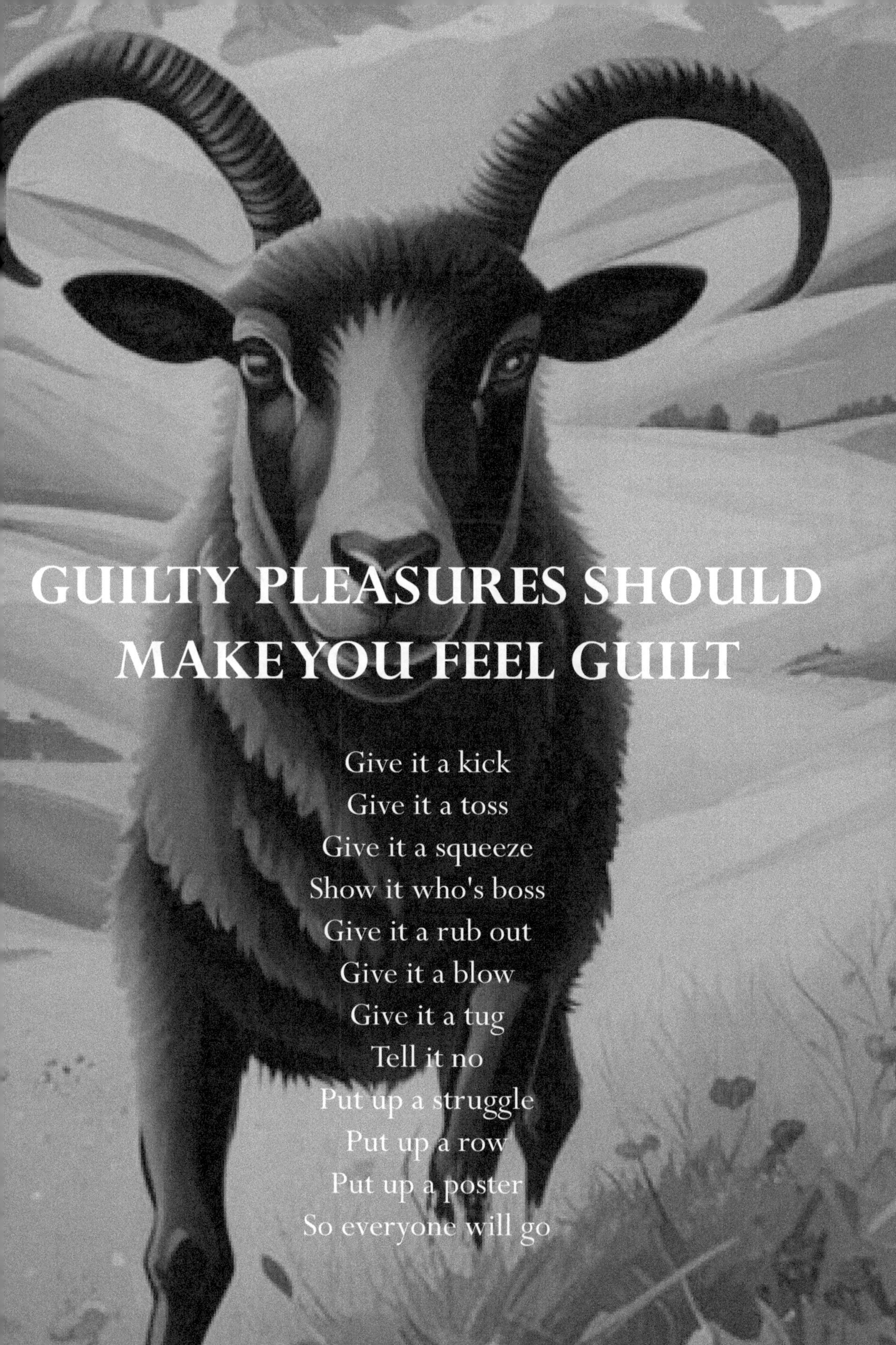

GUILTY PLEASURES SHOULD
MAKE YOU FEEL GUILT

Give it a kick
Give it a toss
Give it a squeeze
Show it who's boss
Give it a rub out
Give it a blow
Give it a tug
Tell it no
Put up a struggle
Put up a row
Put up a poster
So everyone will go

When it's time to sweep the floor
I put the waste under the rug
I hate the dust
I hate the dust
I hate the dust
I hate the dust

WE SIMPLY DON'T KNOW

We simply don't know.
There are things in this universe we cannot fathom
Planes of existence unreachable in our minds
Star-sized computers that look like many-eyed angels
Entire solar systems sentient and alive
Maybe our planet is even alive
Our inability to communicate with objects is likely
A louder statement about our shortcomings
Than some grand commentary on our superiority
In fact, our superiority does not exist
We are always only three successive stumbles away
From being wiped out or dumped in a shallow grave
All our planning and ceremony and ideas of God
Misguided, misinterpreted compensation for feeble brains
This understanding is material in coming to grips with
The fact there are things in the universe we cannot fathom
We simply don't know.

TIME IN A FAMILIAR PLACE

When I walk through the auto doors
I don't know where I am anymore
Everything on the inside is the same so I can walk out in a different time
In a different place under a yet-to-be-remembered sky
The minutes elapse as my memories collapse
Each day I get a little closer
To trading in my will
You know it's not so easy
Traveling the world between automatic doors and the same faces on different bodies
While the location is the same for all of the potties
And when I walk out the doors I am anywhere
I am anyplace
I am anytime
Every time

THEY GO UP!

Hey there dirt ball snot faced kid
Why do you think you can start on top?
You gotta work your way up
You gotta work your way up
The ladder

Hey there dirty snot nosed kid
You are still green behind those ears
You gotta work your way up
You gotta work your way up
The ladder

Don't you know there are a lot of rungs between here and the top?

FURIOUS ANGER

I think that people struggling right now with going back to the "old how" might not even know what's causing the trouble. I suspect this is a direct response to deep-seated trauma. A year filled with unimaginable drama doesn't just magically become swell. You can't just buy pizza and a tee shirt and say "All's well that ends well." People are still trying to reconcile behavior, and vile; regardless of which side of the aisle you reside. The last four years were insane, and people have not begun to understand how the pain may linger for years, like unending rain. Reflecting on it today almost brought me to tears. But my tears were of furious anger. Pent up rage that I'm prepared to take out on a friend, or a stranger. I just need the right reason to make the wrong choice. I'm bored of towing the line with a steady voice. The only lesson I've learned is that we all need to be selfish to a fault. We can't rely on our neighbors to all do their part. In some ways we all lost parts of ourselves we will never get back. It's going to take us a long time to be okay with that.

THAT ALBATROSS AROUND YOUR NECK IS YOUR UNACKNOWLEDGED FEELINGS FOR ME

Do you ever think about me the way I think of you?
Is your life as unfulfilled as mine while I pine?
Maybe that gap could be filled by me?
Maybe the wind your sails are searching for is my stiff breeze?

Have you ever wet your lips with my name on your breath?
Have you ever bit your tongue to keep from whispering for me?
Maybe those steps could be danced together?
Maybe the wind your sails are searching for is my fair weather?

SUCKS

At this age
I have a higher than average
Vacuuming acumen
I do not just suck willie nillie
I know how to suck
Completely
I know how to replace a belt
To tighten
I know how to clean the brush
Enlightened
It's not luck to know how to suck
Experience breeds mastery
Of carpet cleaning and house taskery

THE ROAD

Winners win and losers lose
I can't win away from you
I pass the day with thoughts forgotten
Can't remember what I was going to say
When all the scenery seems the same

Livers live and the dead are dead
Thoughts flow freely from my head
I'll never see where they go
Above the highways they will float
Someone else will take them home
To share anew, they aren't alone

Runners run and sitters sit
I roam about to get my tips
The farther I travel the younger I get
The older I feel the more that I go
I just can't wait to hold you at home
A one-way ticket into your bed
A kiss from you and a place for my head
A break from reality before I do it again

THE AMAZON WOMAN

(READ IN YOUR BEST STEVE IRWIN)

With a savage beauty
More in function than form
She stalks her prey
Completely blended into her surroundings
Masked and robed, ready for battle, she hunts
How far will this particular kill take her?
10 clicks?
40 clicks?
80 clicks?
How many superhighways?
Still she pursues, a relentless machine
Powered by the Three Ines
Adrenaline, caffeine and dopamine force her forward
Urged on by pure instinct
This is.....primal
Bathed in blue, she.... THERE IT IS!
The game is afoot, now, in Sherlockian terms
Her heart quickened by the thrill of engagement
She doesn't need to look at cue cards
This part is memorized
With deft hands and dexterous fingers
She harvests her quarry
In 2-3 business days
A ringing
Her prize
Delivered to her doorstep
A proud cat showing off a mouse

THE TRAIL TO OREGON

Crossing fields at grueling pace
Doctors, merchants, farmers race
Leave in spring and arrive by fall
Reaching Oregon, the dream of all
Adventure and opportunity
The force behind this unity
They'll need to work together
If they intend to beat the weather
Most will leave Missouri
Best if in a hurry
For Indians and snakes are all around
It is miles of prairie to the next town
To hunt, no need for license
You can bring down a bison
With just a couple rounds

However, to the wagon you can only
carry 100 pounds
Now approaching water
In the trailer with wife and daughter
Caulk the wagon and float across
Or hire an Indian to be the boss
Spring rains have risen levels
Those who choose the yellow devil
Are safely ushered to western bank
Those who caulked were doomed and
sank
Quickly buried without applause
Many more will die for this cause
It may be from dysentery
Or gored to death by something hairy

Catch a fever or bite from skunk
Or aforementioned wagon sunk
More ways to die than clothes for fashion
All these miles on meager rations
Still two rivers needed to cross
Sacrifice at any cost
Mother, daughter, in a grave
Telling junior to be brave
Having crossed the Snake it's to the Dalles
Still many chances left for falls
Oxen tired wheels broke
Indian stole the last wagon yolk
Through dogged determination

These pioneers crisscross the nation
It's now September, supplies so low
There's only one way left to go
One last caulk then in the drink
Dodging rocks and on the brink
The cool breeze off the water
Justice for all who nature slaughtered
Gentle current guides to shore
More beautiful than all the lore
Three of five have made it through
Now to build and start anew
Still more wagons rolling on
Risking all on the trail to Oregon

Author Note: These wagons killed me.
"Hey AI, you know how to draw a wagon, right? RIGHT?"

EVERYTHING I'D RATHER DO THAN EAT AT THE RESTAURANT ATTACHED TO BASS PRO SHOPS

I'd wear sandals to a music fest
Brush my teeth with Tilapia Crest
Make eye contact with lemon zest
I'd call Nickelback the best
Then run through Merle Hay Mall undressed
Take an arrow through the breast
Receive a foot into my nuts
Have a killer remove my guts
Sell my house, move to huts
Stick my tongue in filthy butts
Watch all seasons of Jersey Shore
Slam my hand in Buick's door
Go to jail for being poor
Wear white pants like trust fund boor
Hang myself with cashmere scarf
Into my face I'd shovel barf
Drink piss straight from someone's south
Take a gentleman in the mouth
Eat some boogers, eat a shoe
Wipe my ass then eat that too
All these things are much preferred
To breaking fast inside that turd
It's certainly hyperbole but I don't give two fucks
You'll never catch me eating at Bass Pro's Uncle Buck's

AN EXCELLENT POINT WAS MADE

The 'smartest' man in the god damned place
Sure looks good with egg on his face.
All the books a body could read
Can't make up for sensibility.
This meeting could use brevity
Of which I'll ask with levity,
My life will end before this wraps
Is my whole existence just a series of craps?
Devour time from 8 to 5
Then shit it out before it's 9
Come back in the following day
Not a single excellent point was made

NEVERENDING FEEDBACK LOOP

Fairest maiden wouldst thou go
Aboard the ship then down below
A secret tryst, remove thy clothes
Unleash your woman as manhood grows

Bend thy spine to see the port
Alas you are a savory tort!
With wit and wile to match your rear
Such kiss and touch and nibbled ear

So sit you coyly on that bench
And meet my kiss, you fearless wench
And whence this poem has reached the end
I implore you, start again!

MATH FACTS

I never knew after five years of being discrete
The answer would leap out
My calculations came out with the right answers this time
Without looking in the back of the book
Just don't ask me to show my work
I'm a good estimator
After one date I saw
Our Venn diagrams
More a single circle
I managed to figure out the proof without geometry
Instead, through constant study
I'm not a fast learner
But I know that if your legs form a triangle
I want to find the hypotenuse
I think your heart, eyes, brain and smile
Make up the quadratic love equation
I know sometimes I'm a square
I would give you any shape
For just a small area in your heart
Even a parallelo-
Grandma says you are a good catch
I want to solve for X

EAT YOU OUT OF HOUSE AND HAT

Fickle like an aging cat
I'll eat you out of house and hat
Incredulous, I'll swallow lids
Surprised I lost in betting this
One-million-dollar goal by age 30
Finally became debt free by nearly 40
Goals I've set just for myself
Placed upon the highest shelf
I've managed money very badly
Instead of fiscal smarts and savvy
Fancy dinners multiplied
Not choosing the veg instead of fried
Luckily housed thanks to refi
Haven't failed although I've tried
Dumb mistakes and almost bust
Lost my faith and all self-trust
Through it all life's been cordial
Sometimes I wish for magic portals
Not to gold or life aplomb
Instead freedom from doldrums and ho hums
Not to silver or platinum plated
But just enough to be satiated
Unfound, these portals don't exist
Just more hard work and shaking fists
That's alright, I'll bide my time
Punch that clock for overtime
I may be a dickhead jerk
But I will never be outworked
Fickle like an aging cat
I'll eat you out of house and hat

I'M STILL JENNY FROM THE WRITER'S BLOCK

The God damn words
Escape me
They aren't gone, I mean, I can see 'em
Sitting there like a rabbit
Remember when we were kids?
And we did the kid things kids did?
Grandpa told me if I could sprinkle salt on a rabbit's tail
I could catch it
But I'm belligerently stupid
I thought the salt would stop the rabbit from running
But he meant that if you could
Get.
      Close
          Enough
              To salt it
                Then
          You
     Could
          Get
          Close
             Enough

                    TO CATCH IT!

So I sit here
Salting these words
Hoping they somehow arrange themselves on this paper
Like so many rabbits
But they might as well be wounds
Sometimes I can carry words
The way J-Lo can carry a tune
But today,
Today, the words are rabbits
And I can't catch a fucking cold

Sometimes the simplest things

                      Feel like a wake service

          The obligation I have to do

          Even though it's almost unbearable

Sometimes the dishes

                      Are like leaving work an hour early

                      So I can drive two hours west

This lawn that needs mowed

                      A semi-distant relative to whom I must pay respects

                      I see family and friends I haven't seen in years

          More like strangers

                      Even needing to introduce myself as my father's son

Soooooo teeeeeedious..............

                      ....this laundry pile is like a corpse

One time viewing before I stuff them away

          Condolences for your loss

                      A father or daughter suddenly gone like my ambition

          Standing around because I can't leave yet

                      Making small talk about how quick he or she went

                      Or how his or her story is such a tragedy

Sweeping, dusting, vacuuming all around me

          Like strangers

          Like distant relatives

Sometimes the simplest things

                      Feel like a wake service

LIFE'S PERFECT BALANCE

Through my unbalances
I achieve perfect balance
It's a recipe borne of inequity
From the layman's eyes
But I'm still Nerfed
Sociopathic tendencies
Seasoned with empathy
Enough drive to outclass most mortals
Enough self-awareness to sow seeds of self-doubt
Equal parts elitist and depressive
Panic laced with vanity
Hubris for my brain and pubis
Mixed with casual anger to keep fans and haters on eggshells
Always simmering for no good reason
These two devils on my shoulders in constant treason
Commiseration between miseries
Never a conscious plan
But I always end up where I'm going
Handling praise the same way I handle defeat
That's what keeps me on my feet
Instead of swinging in the barn
Or making bathtub toast
This is me: equal parts self-deprecation and boast
Two devils who, when left unchecked
Create life's perfect balance

THE ROMANTICISM OF THE BIRTH OF J. HELEN CHRIST IN A BARN

Away in a manger no room for crib
But there's a nice pile of shit
And some straw,
I call dibs

Our heroine Mary the purist of lore
Either that or dear Mary is a first-rate lying whore
Who made a cuck of Joseph, poor
Documented forevermore

Three men showed up eager
with gifts to bestow
Too bad there's no Maury
No tests, and no show

If not truly pure
Our sweet Mary goes hard in the paint
Even more reason
To make Joe a saint

Then quickly to donkey
Then away in a burst
Our Mary is either
The best or the worst

Joseph my man
Deserves our respect
Regardless of cuckoldship
By her side he never left

Of one thing's for certain
I approve JC's style
Even if his bio father
Is an angelic pedophile

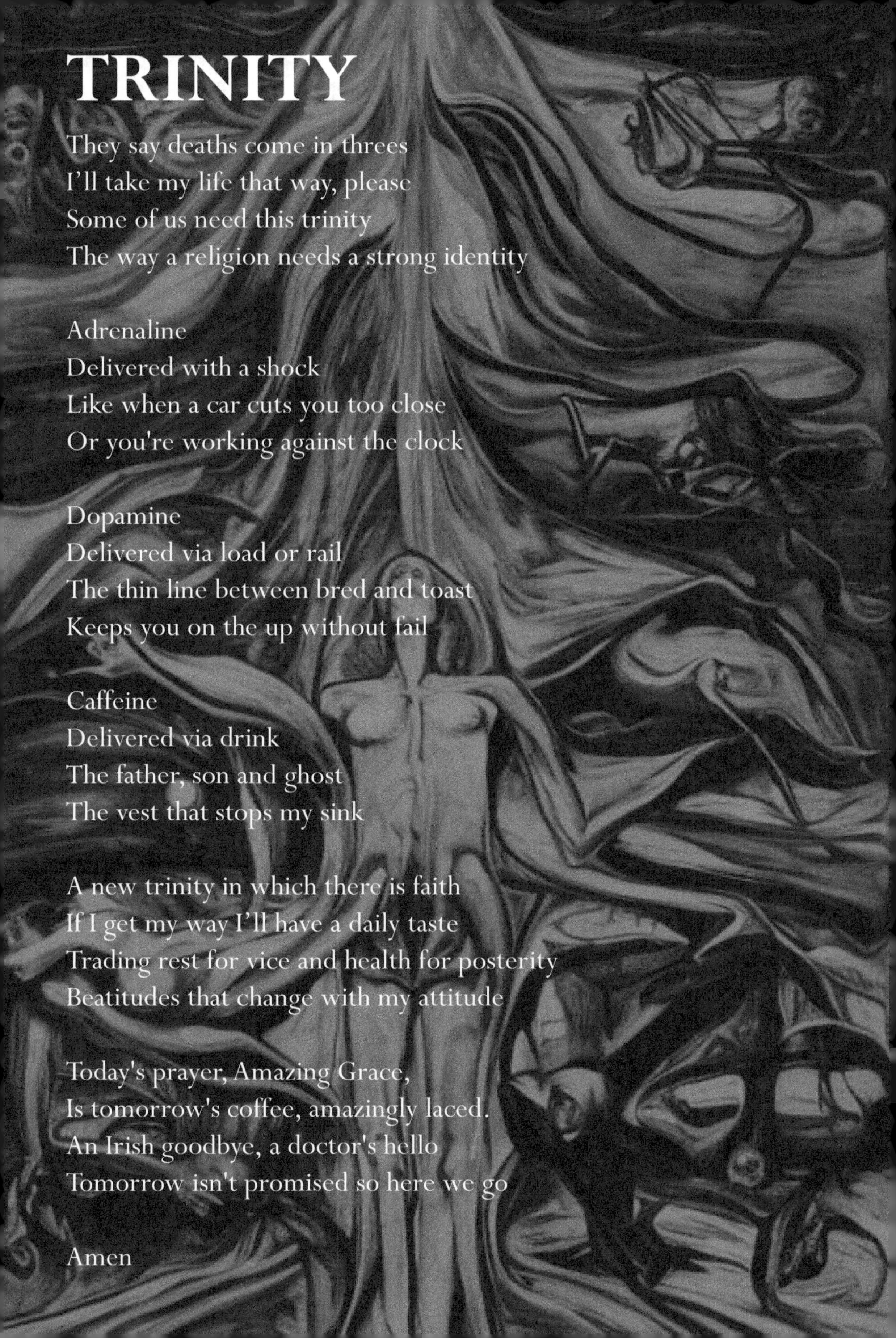

TRINITY

They say deaths come in threes
I'll take my life that way, please
Some of us need this trinity
The way a religion needs a strong identity

Adrenaline
Delivered with a shock
Like when a car cuts you too close
Or you're working against the clock

Dopamine
Delivered via load or rail
The thin line between bred and toast
Keeps you on the up without fail

Caffeine
Delivered via drink
The father, son and ghost
The vest that stops my sink

A new trinity in which there is faith
If I get my way I'll have a daily taste
Trading rest for vice and health for posterity
Beatitudes that change with my attitude

Today's prayer, Amazing Grace,
Is tomorrow's coffee, amazingly laced.
An Irish goodbye, a doctor's hello
Tomorrow isn't promised so here we go

Amen

THE HIGH ACTIVIST

When the High Activist starts to make a point, it goes
On
And on
And on
And on
And on
And on
And on
And on
And on
Andon
Ndon
Ndon
Ndon
A dona
Don
Don Knotts
Adonal foyle
A fucking roa-ad
A stacked to-ad
Donna Reed
To the window
To the wall
Till I hang myself in the hall
And on nd onnaksosalsbbefhchsiajoawkskskdkskkssksks

Christ. I'd rather talk to a vegan.

CHARCUTERIE

Occasionally,
Life kicks your ass so brutally,
You feel like the charcuterie.
Thinly sliced….served, exposed on a plank
When life lights you on fire, who's to thank?
When you did the right thing but got punished?
Fair play is rubbish.
Stoop low if you must.
It's the only way to win back trust.
Stand tall if you can.
It's the only way to stick it to the man.

POWERING THE TOWNSHIP

When I know you want to fuck
It's like electricity
When I know you want to fuck me
It's over in one, two, three
When you know I want to fuck you
It's "Go fly a kite, and remember key!"

MIXED TAPES

The thrill is in the time we waste
At arm's length instead of giving chase
The perfect rhyme stuck in our throats
Singing off time but it's the perfect note
We'll stand above the precipice
Instead of holding hands, we're balling fists
Hearts as one yet still divided
Mutual feelings but actions unrequited

THE VIVID SOUNDS
OF IMAGINATION

Do people imagine me fucking
The way I imagine them fucking
We all do it so why be ashamed
Everyone wants to rut
I'm sure in our professional exchanges
You've made some of your intimate noises
I'm sure I've shown what sounds I emphasize
In jest or subconscious
I don't mean anything by it
I'm just curious how people fuck
The same way one might tour a factory
Or learn about the past in a museum

Of all the demons I could have asked for
You're the hardest to keep in check
Symbiotic now
To kill you is to kill me
So much of my anatomy
Overgrown with your thorns
But I think I've found an antidote
I may not be able to kill you
But I can keep you at bay
I can play my demons against each other
The politician's way
Teaching old me new tricks
The taste of blood fades
With fewer wounds to lick

ELIXIR

You linger
Me wrapped
Your fingers
Gracefully guide
Your music
Quiet singer
You resonate
My fixer
Your love
Sweet elixir
My wounds
You're ginger
My dressing
You configure
Slow to heal
You quicken
My blood
You thicken
My paint chipped
You coat
My poison
You antidote

REV

Where do you go to feel?
What are your revs? What helps you heal?
I'm sure your heart
Could use a jump start
What kind of base shit gives you the get?
What kind of seedy feelings make you wet?
Any kind of dampness will do
Lust or tears
Just whisper something
In my ear
Tearing through life on an empty tank
What a shit way to live
You can't give something when there's nothing left
But I'll give your engine a crank
Maybe you're missing a part
There's got to be some way to jump start your heart
Doesn't anything make you rev?

APATHY

I can feel your weight on my shoulder
I can faintly hear your whispers
Coaxing me into your embrace
Nothing is more dangerous
Than your whispers
You are a tiny Bruno Mars
Trying to get me in the backseat of your car
It's a twenty-four-hour hard sell
You thrive on everything passé
I can feel my soul being depressed by your weight
With a sculptor's deftness
You bore your holes
Bullseyes through my ambitions
You strike the right tone
You spin sophisticated fictions
I want to buy what you sell
But I have to resist
Like Rocky-Creed II, I must persist
These ropes won't climb themselves
Without action, words won't write these spells
Clothes aren't self-folding
Dirty dishes aren't self-demolding
The things I want and need
In constant battle with your hopes and dreams

The secret to life
Just give up
Can't be knocked down
When you're not at the top
No reason to try
If you don't go, you don't need to stop
Things are just things
Once you give them up freely
Freedom will ring
No more anxiety
Not one single care
Goodbye, all the pretense
Poof! Thin air.
You can just be a number
Be an also ran
Yes, I hear your whispers
Three feet from my hands

THAT TIME YOU ACCIDENTALLY SAW MY SOUL

We'd just finished dinner
And we walked out of the restaurant with our heads held high
Made our way to the car on a chilly October night
We got in the car and died
Our brave faces walking out had been a lie
We've never undressed in front of each other
Never seen our skin unclothed
But that was the first time we saw each other naked
Utterly ashamed and defeated
Neither of us had ever seen anyone so exposed
As I started the car I turned my head forward
In the glass reflection I could see us
Cast like Adam and Eve from Eden
We had just eaten, gorged on forbidden fruit until we were full
That night was the time we unexpectedly showed each other our souls
In a time where neither of us had ever been so fragile
We drove around for a little while
As we helped each other redress inside our minds
Through the Chicago city streets we drove in silence
Recovering from being stripped with such violence
By the time the evening came to an end
We were disheveled, but mostly clothed again
That was the night we became something different than just friends
I've never been in any other situation
Where I could actually feel what another person felt
None of my former flames ever felt this same way
None of my closest pals had weathered
What it's like to drown together
The two of us shared thoughts and fears on a higher level
For a few hours we were possessed by the same devil
I'm glad when we were both ripped asunder
We had each other to keep from going under
Instead of giving up resigned to total loss
We found out we were cut from the same cloth
Whether we drift apart or if we stay close
I'll always be thankful we shared a little bit of our souls

ANTIDOTE

When the sweet nothings on my shoulder get too loud
She knows how to calm them down
When anger and apathy get the best of me
Everything is going dark
She knows how to shine a light
She is tinder for my spark
She knows how to set me right
No weight on my shoulders is too great
With her in my sights

Be cheap with your time
The way misers are cheap with their dime
You can mint more coin
But the minutes are ticking on your loins
Screw the age-old adages
"A rainy day is coming"
"Best save all your money so you don't end up thumbing"
Listen, no day is promised
If forced to choose today's adventure vs tomorrow indentures
I'm out the door and in the whip
Champing at the bit
Like an excitable pup
Like an addict who can't get enough
Keep one eye on the future and two on the now
Don't pass on a story for financial glory
A lonely pile of money is boring

STINGY

I'm stingy with my appetite
I'm not just going to stuff my face with any shit
I don't want to awaken in a ditch
Realization I'm headed out setting in
Only for my last thought to be chagrin
Disgusted my final meal was Jason's Deli
Floating, below average in my dying belly
Embarrassed for what the coroner will find
Ashamed I slummed my last meal for the sake of time
Only you've got your back (and stomach!)
So I implore you
Be stingy with your appetite
Be judicious with what you deem delicious
Lest your last meal be regret
Lying in a ditch

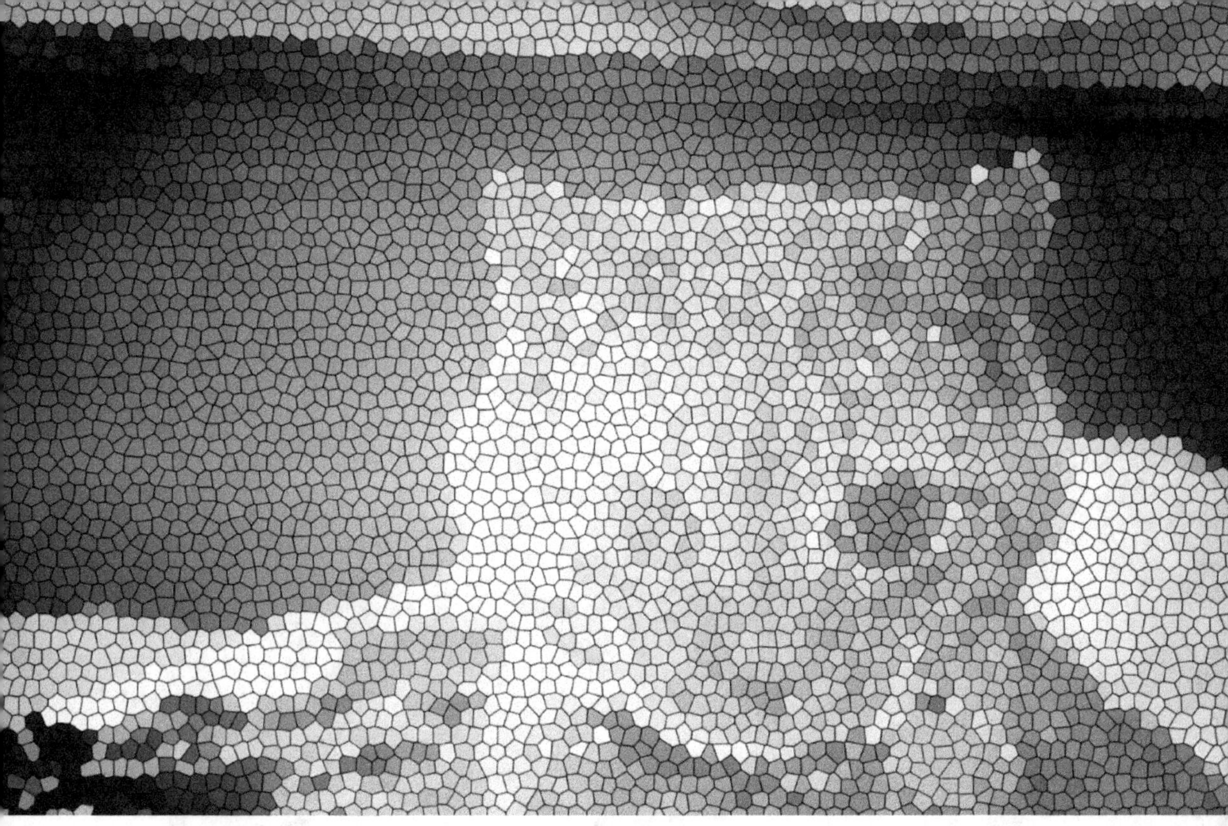

THEM: "DO YOU THINK YOU GUYS WILL HAVE KIDS?"

ME: "THAT'S A HARD NO FROM ME, DOG."

One of the shittiest feelings yet
When I took kitty to the vet
She's fine, this one ends happily
But so scared, she shook so violently
She hates the car, she hates new things
Her kitty shouts could rival trains
Her little voice, so raw and dry
Almost makes me want to cry
Then just like that, the vet is done
Back to the car and on the run
Safe at home she snuggles in
If I'm like this with a cat
It's a good thing I don't have kids

NORMAL FRUIT

Apples from a broken tree
Won't make themselves into delicacies
They need a little help
And they needed some luck
To go from rotting on the vine
To state fair prize
Maybe sauce, or some apple butter
A nice pie or delectable crisp
We only took the ones still on the tree
How many more apples with potential
Lie rotting on the ground for the worms
Feasts for hungry animals

BEACON

The years come and go
My feelings stay
Day one as much as one day
You're a beacon
And a home
When I feel like a stranger
You're the one who helps me know
My fortification
My first and last defense
I strive to do better
In your presence
Even when times were
A little bitter
Life threw lemons
But we're not quitters
Together we stir the drink
If it doesn't fit our lives
We'll pour it down the sink
You're my better and my best
Provided we keep trying
Love will do the rest

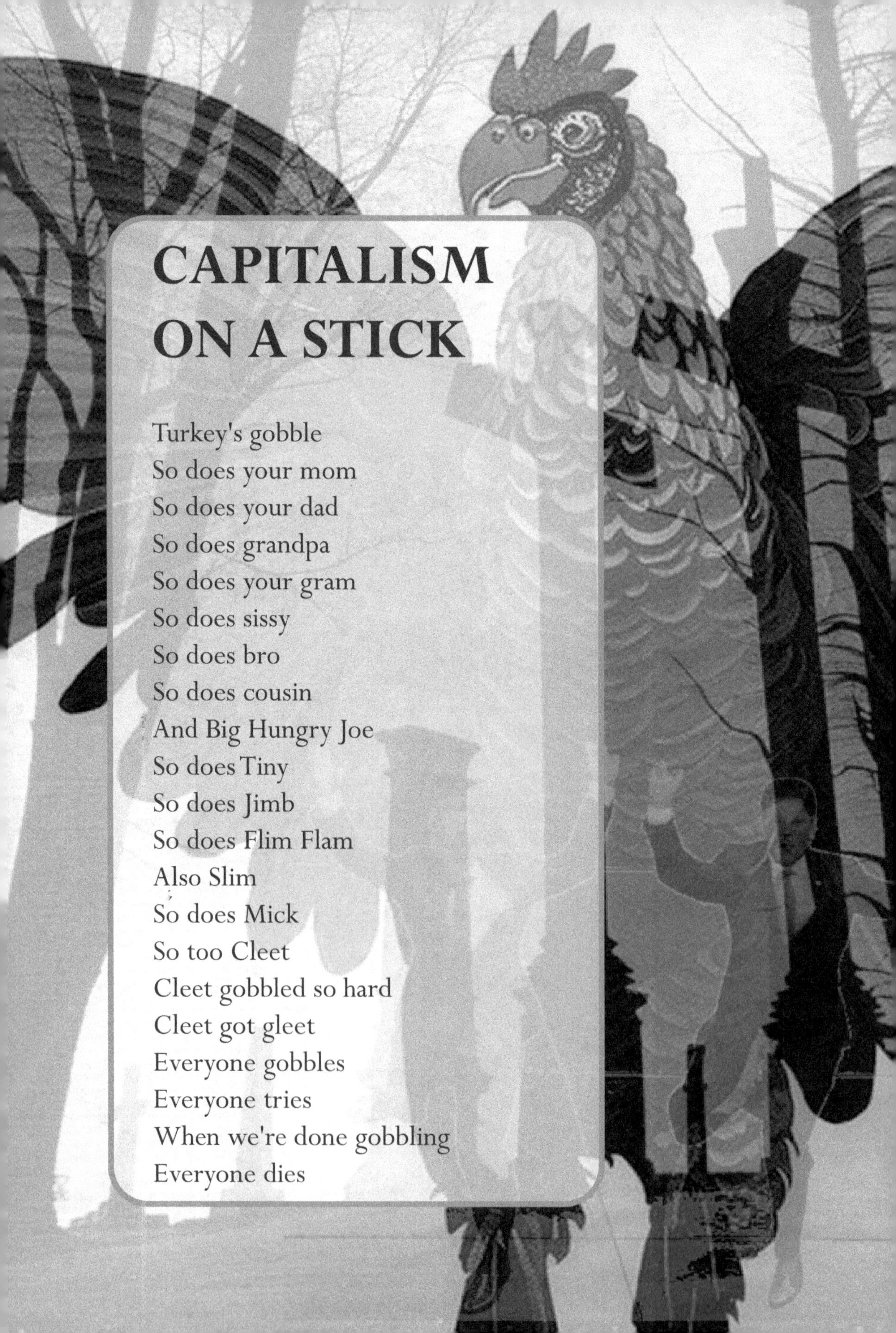

CAPITALISM ON A STICK

Turkey's gobble
So does your mom
So does your dad
So does grandpa
So does your gram
So does sissy
So does bro
So does cousin
And Big Hungry Joe
So does Tiny
So does Jimb
So does Flim Flam
Also Slim
So does Mick
So too Cleet
Cleet gobbled so hard
Cleet got gleet
Everyone gobbles
Everyone tries
When we're done gobbling
Everyone dies

THIS IS YOUR INVITATION

You can't pick when the planets align
Whether it's fate or chance
When the tune gets called, you gotta dance
When the baton gets passed
You gotta haul ass
Labor's fruits won't cook themselves
When the wind is fair, you must set sail
If they pass you a cape, it's yours to don
If they pass the mic, sing your song

THE GRAND MARSHAL

Getting old is a great big suck.
Everything I have still works,
But watching 80 year olds fumble and tumble – it hurts.
"I fell yesterday"
What could I say?
What *should* I say?
"Be glad you aren't in the ground today?"
"Be glad you aren't the Grand Marshal in the hearse parade?"
Hit him with two "that's crazies?"
That seems insincere and lazy.
It isn't crazy.
Not when muscle and brain are respectively ruined and hazy.
The fog of years plus atrophy are the leading cause of familial catastrophes.
I want to go out with a bang - literally or figuratively.
This getting old isn't my thing
But for now, everything here "works"

LATE CAPITALISM

All of my monies
Committed to bank
Safe from a heist
Safe from a spank
Instead all my clams
Turned into chowder
No more house
No more white powder
Bankrupt and defeated
Off to a cliff
Soon to be yeeted

THE BIG NEWS

I thought as much
When we set it up
That you'd have news
And it would be good
And it was good
And timely, too!
And we're all happy
So happy for you

THE TASTE OF SUNSHINE

What does sunshine taste like?
A really fresh smoothie that's so bright and vibrant but warms you up on the inside
A big juicy tomato the size of a softball that takes up a whole piece of bread
A spicy mango salsa that explodes with freshness and the chip is so crisp it echoes
when you bite through
Sun tastes the way chorizo sauté fills the room with spice and punches you with a
robust flavor on a tortilla
Sunlight fills a room the same way roasted garlic smells
It's a fresh crispy carrot
It's a piece of raspberry pie with rich ice cream
And the pie has only been out of the oven for a few minutes

A HEAVY WALK TURNED LIGHTER

On a walk yesterday
Feeling heavy for no good reason
Just, like, heavy? You know? With thoughts?
I'm not religious. I gave that up for lent
Years ago
But I do like J. Helen Christ
I like his style and his words
I think emulating him is just the ticket
But it struck me on a heavy walk
As my feet kept time to the sounds around me
Even if I don't believe in fairy tales
I can make the characters whatever I want
What if I replaced Jesus with something else?
What if……
…Hope is always with you
…Love is the alpha and the omega
…Only through kindness will you achieve eternal life
And if the hope, love and kindness we share
Lives on in the hearts of others?
My steps became lighter
As the sun peeked out from behind a cloud

I brought a gun to a word fight
I took a bat to a knife fight
I took a balloon to an airplane contest
I took a squat when it was time to bench press
You brought a donkey to a horse race
You drove a bike to a car race
You brought a chair to take a stand
You gave a foot when asked to shake hands

Baby, we were meant for each other!

SPILL THAT TEA

I got a ring ring ring ring ringing in my pants
But I'm not gonna answer, it's potential spam
I got a buzz buzz buzz buzz buzzing in my shorts
No doubt someone trying to give me reports
Or maybe retorts
Or maybe cohorts
Trying to spill the tea
Another busy bee divulging secrets to me
Another loose lipped acquaintance
And for hot gossip I have patience
I need that juice
I need those deets
Say the words loudly and on repeat
Oh my goodness
It was all in my brain
No one actually called me
Because I'm so lame

BREADS AND COOKIES

Breads
Breads and cookies
Cookies cakes and pies
Jam them all into my face
Until I nearly die
Until I lose a foot
There's so many I want to try
So sweet and fluffy
So rich and dense
I should go downtown right now
Give a baker half my rent
Thirteen baker's dozens
That's a paycheck that's well spent

Breads and cookies
Cookies cakes and pies
I will never not eat sweets
Ignore my doctor's lies
Diabetes
I'm sure that goes away
I can drive a little scooter
Or get a wooden leg
Chew on a bear claw gingerly
While I hobble on my peg
Maybe I can make it
Out of sugar formed and pressed
Eat some cake until I'm tired
Then eat some while I rest
Breads, breads and cookies
Simply are the best

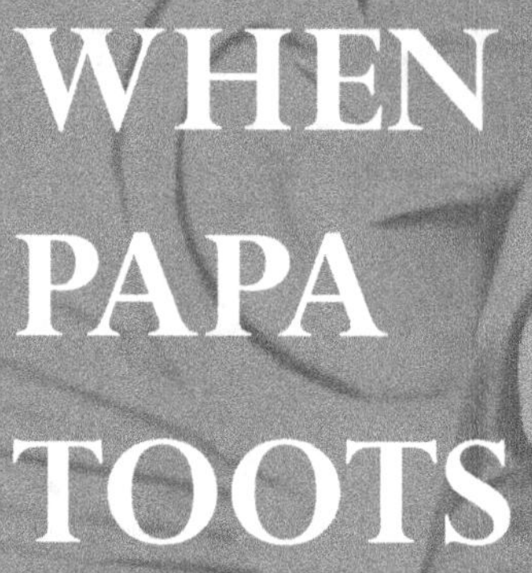

WHEN PAPA TOOTS

If papa toots
And blows a hole
Through his chair
To floor below
Do you laugh?
Do you cry?
Depending on smell
You may die!
Or worse, live!
To survive dad's toot
Fate worse than death
When stuck in a car
No fresh breath
No escape
Watery eyes
Smell coats like paint
Thank you papa
You ruined our life
You ruined the seat
No, no papa!
Please no repeat!

THE PRICE OF ADMISSION

How much cash would it take?
To get you to eat an entire cake?
64 slices in a standardized sheet,
Immediate diabetes, lose your feet!
How many monies for you to chug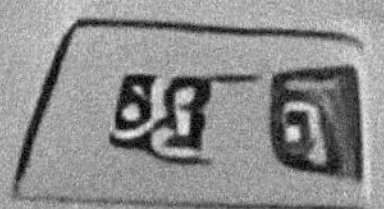
32 pounds of gravy from lug?
The gravy is thick and the gravy is cold.
But for the right price, will you be bold?
Please tell me how many duckets,
For you to drink mustard straight from a bucket?
Only five gallons when filled to the brim.
If the price is right, will you do it on a whim?
What is the count of currency clams?
I want you to swallow an entire yam.
Can you python your human throat?
Is there a price? Would you choke?
For $22 and $.85
And two months' wages and three months' rent,
Could I get you to eat an old shoe?
Is there enough? What can I get you to do?
I think everyone has a price.
And making money is certainly nice!
Don't do dares that will make you die.
Some things aren't worth making mom cry.
Sometimes rent isn't worth mother's lament

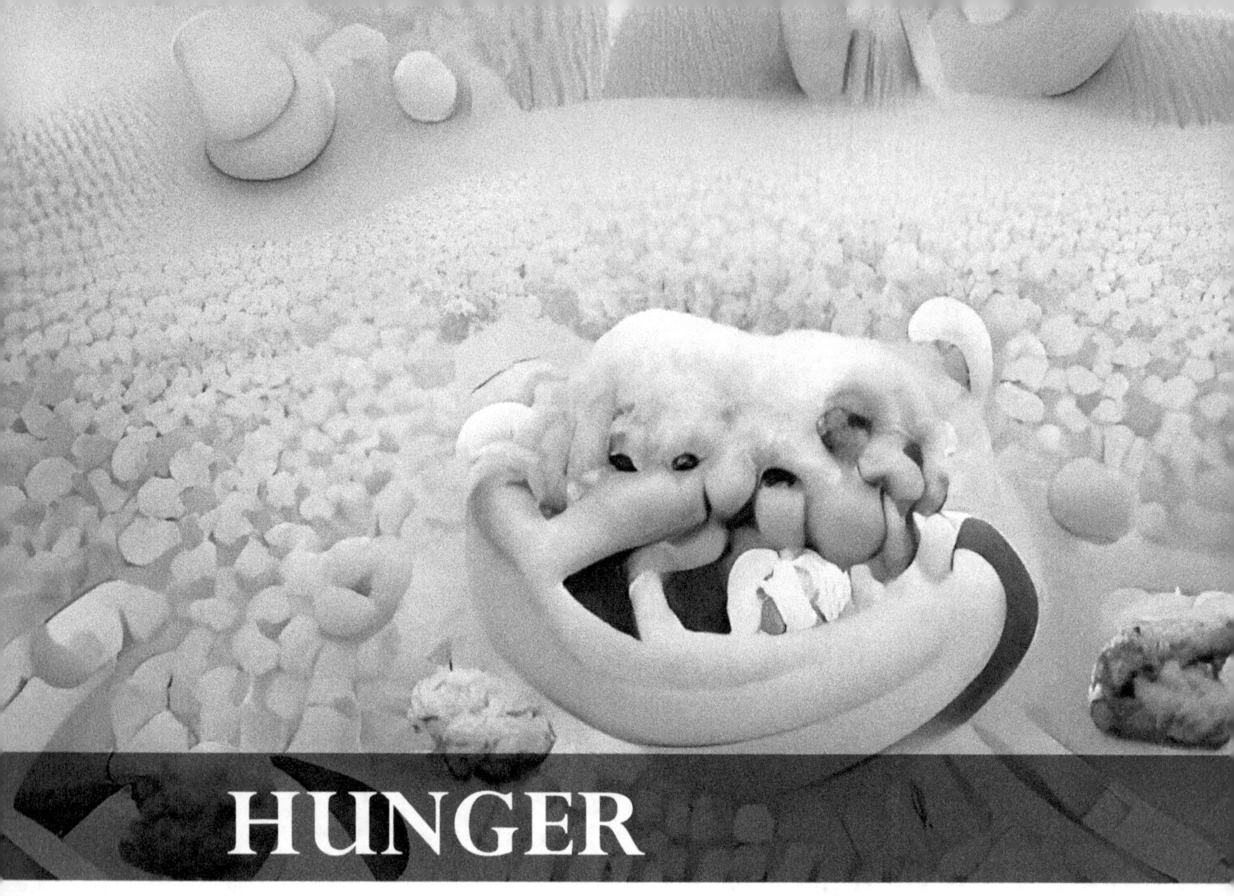

HUNGER

The neighbors got a puppy
It's a precious sight
A little ball of caramel fur
Who doesn't bark or bite
I catch myself just watching
As it rolls around and plays
If the world really goes kaput
I may eat that dog someday

LUNCH DATE

Mom and dad had a wrestling match
They seemed to lose their clothes
You were so naive you told your friends
Now the whole town knows
What your folks are doing
Instead of making lunch
And the reason you got a Nintendo Switch
If I have half a hunch

Note: Absolutely I gave the AI a prompt for
Norman Rockwell. I came up with this
whole poem based on "What if Norman
Rockwell painted a nooner?"

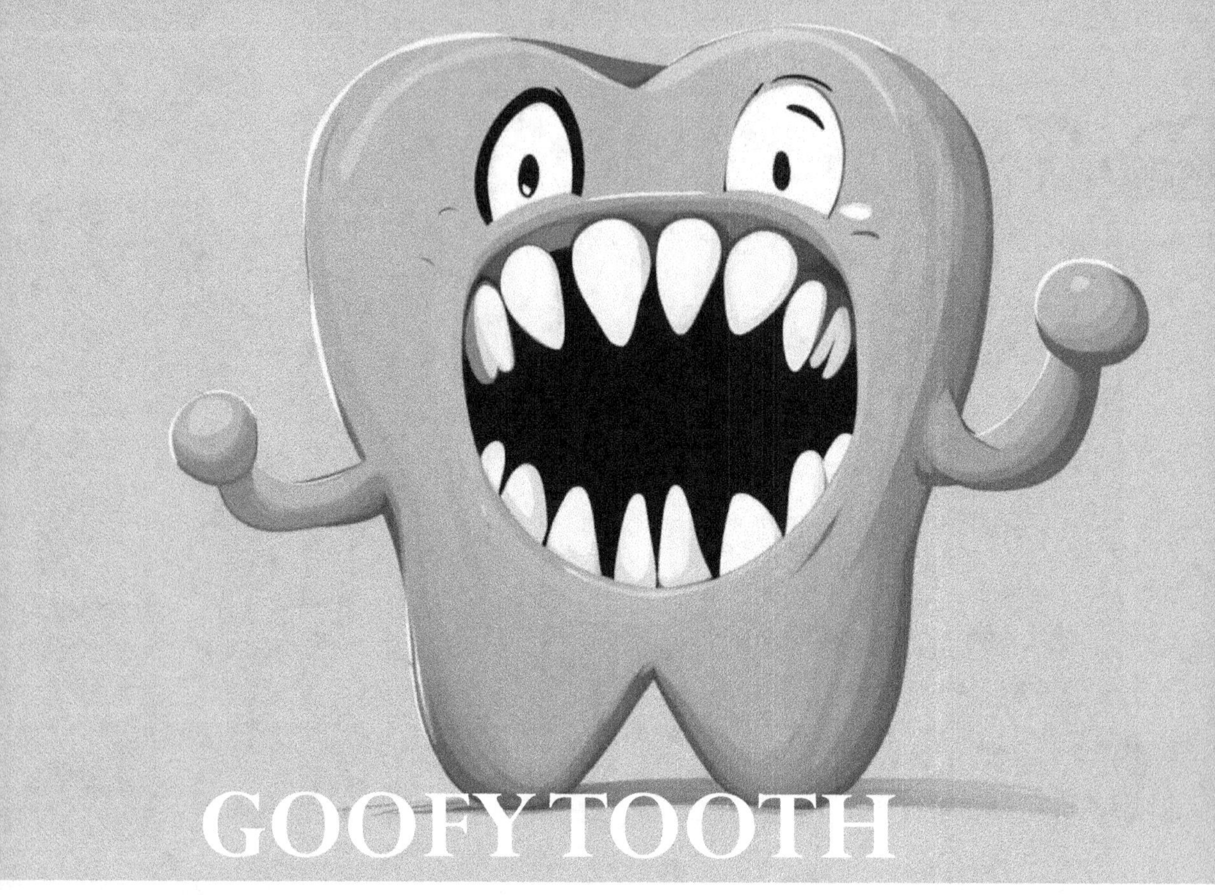

If you got a goofy tooth
Longer than a finger
And it precludes you from eating cobbed corn
Or being a famous singer
Don't let anyone disparage
You or your goofy tooth
You still have things to offer
That's the honest truth
Maybe you can help them
Open up a can
And maybe you can use your tooth
To scare away a mean old man
I hope you keep your tooth
Until you're very old
You can hand it down to your kids
If you get it coated in gold!

HAPPY TRAILS, FLORENCE JEAN

I started the morning with a chip and it went downhill from there. As I fist-fought my way through meetings and wrestled the gator that is and always will be my temper, I countered my carbonated blood with more coffee and a bullpen rotation of ibuprofen and acetaminophen. This helped back me off a ledge, but I didn't feel right. Didn't feel right until nine at night.

I ended the day the next day. It was well after one before I finally was in a place I thought I could sleep. As I lie there tossing and turning, I could feel anxiety expanding like a balloon in my abdomen. Awful, horrible images kept popping into my brain the way images change on a slideshow screensaver. This continued, building in tension and need until 2:30, at which point I promptly fell asleep.

When I woke up, I learned you had died in the night.

MAMBO #6

A little bit of nihilism in my life
A little bit of looting by my side
A little bit of anarchy is all I need
A little bit of bullshit is what I see
A little bit of cover-up in the sun
A little bit of protest all night long
A little bit of fuck you, here I am
A little bit of you makes me take a stand

Jump up and down and march all around
Shake your fist to the marching sound
Time to stand our collective ground
Take one step left and none steps right
Time to make people listen even if it takes a fight
Burn one Target then burn another one twice
And if it looks like the Boston Tea Party
Then you are doing it right

I CAN'T
BREATHE

It's always throats
Never handshakes
It's always bullets
Never.....

...... never open hearts

VIBING

The weed eater had significant vibration and my fingers felt like they were on acid and my arms ached like a bodybuilder and when I needed new blades I replaced the little dealies that go betwixt the blades and then when I fired it up again that baby sang like famous divas belting out the hits and sliced through the lush spring greenery the way a newer model Cadillac glides effortlessly down the Pacific Coast Highway on a sunny day with my girl

THE BI-POLAR EXPRESS

Up then down
Then down then downer
Then near elation
Then near conflagration
Then wishing for conflagration
Then having conflagration under skin
A white-hot flame
Ready to commit sin
Ready to release the flames within
Ready to burn it down and start again
Then back up
Up up and away
Don't like right now?
Just wait a day

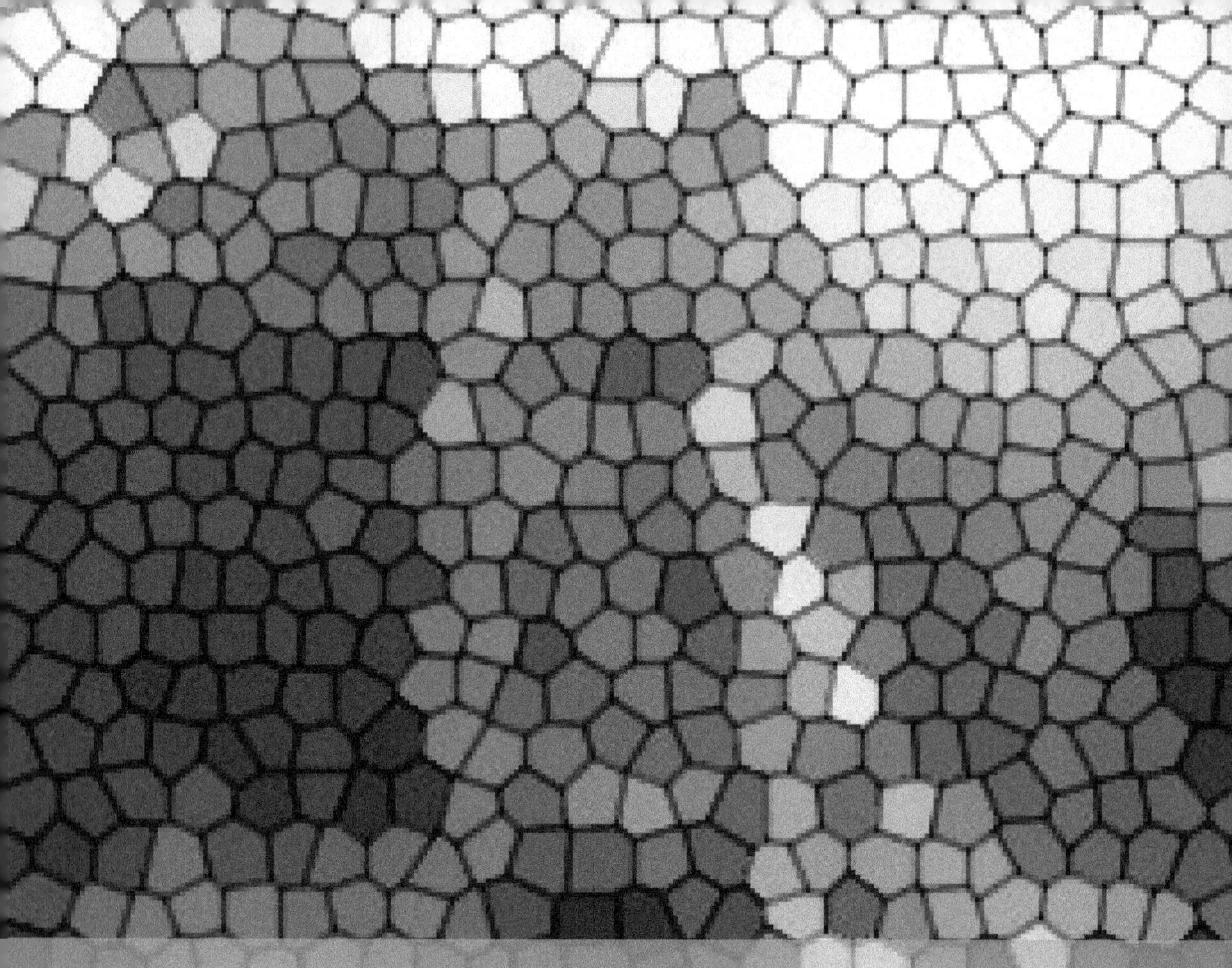

WHEN MAXIE MET PUMA

You.
A tiny, woe begotten thing.
Pitifully huddled.
Nearly frozen.
Days, hours, or maybe just minutes away from becoming owl food.
You didn't say anything.
But we looked at each other.
We made eye contact.
And that was it.
When I needed a friend the
few times I've felt terribly alone,
you knew and you joined me.
We sit together staring straight ahead.
Your vibrations like an emotional massage,
working out my tension and calming me down.
You are a good kitty.
You are a good friend.

FLESHING vs. FLUSHING

When you have a plan
Just the skeleton
Start by adding ligaments
Muscle laced with veins
Veins filled with blood
Blood filled with oxygen
A heart to pump and kidneys to filter
The final step: lightning rod's gift
Breathing life into your creation
Now you feel a sense of elation
That's fleshing a plan

When you have a plan
A fifteen-inch turd
The parts stink
It might look colorful
The bits of corn simply waste ideas -
Ideas undigested and evacuated
As they should
A series of pipes and sewer lines
Get rid of it.
It stinks.
That's flushing a plan

HOW MANY BUTTHOLES?

Everyone has a butthole
Some people have two
Imagine!
Every time they open their mouth
An endless cascade of crumbling road apples
Tumbled forth like a beautiful brown and green fountain
Baby birding you with uneatable words
The faint smell of hooved animal excrement
Lingering in every room they've visited
I wonder more than is healthy for me:
Is it diet? Are they just regurgitating?
The fruit of poorly stewarded lands,
Or is it innate?
An endless factory within.
Working three shifts
Ensuring they can salt the fields of every conversation
Lacing the crops of collaboration with sickening bacteria
Poisoning the streams of discourse
And most importantly
Am I one of them?
Everyone has a butthole
Some people have two

SECOND HALF

I have this theory and I am sticking to it
That I still have half a life to live
That doesn't mean that
I am waiting
To
Try
To do the things
I want to try to accomplish
It just means that I get to start the
Second half with a brain that isn't made

Of mush

WELL, I GUESS WE'LL HAVE TO EAT OUR WAY OUT

Eating my way through the pandemic
What a swell way to die
Not from cough or COVID symptoms
But chicken thigh and pot pie
Ice cream, cookies, pies, braids and cus(tard)
I'll die before I let quarantine beat us

Eating our way through lockdown
Growing big, not strong
Our will to eat hasn't lessened
Bought Masterclass just for chef lessons
Watch a few clips between umami bites
This is how we whittle nights

Eating our way through endless weeks
So desperate for newness
We've started cooking leeks
Butter on everything, including roast beets
And a sigh after each big meal
"Now I just need a little something sweet"

WWJHCD

What would J. Helen say?
When you cherry pick his words
While you raw dog your way
Through the grocery aisles
Breathing out your mouth
Threatening to share this curse
And send your loved ones to deepest South
I hope someone punches you in the lips
Mangled flesh stuck to their knuckles
A full-on rocker from rolling hips
I pray to see your knees buckle
As you reel from getting rocked
You can't be troubled to help the cause?
Even threat to loved ones
Doesn't give you pause?
You aren't a martyr; lives aren't something you barter
You're really just a jerk
You don't care about wellbeing
You just want people to go back to work
So you can have your convenience
Just prolonging the misery
You may as well just be Pence

I AM A GUIDERAIL

I fly by the seat of my pants, meaning…

No plan.   But there's always a vision.

Of words to come.   Of actions to take.

None of this was how I saw it going.

A bowling alley. Empty, save for me and pins….

Every lane has kiddie bumpers in the gutters.

I man all lanes.   Back and forth.

Spinning balls towards pins.   You think I'm in control.

But I am not in control.

I am just a guiderail.

I move quickly. No stopping to admire work…..

No savoring the journey. There's always another ball.

Always another alley. Always something to correct.

I've got to keep them moving.   Pressing forward.

Only now when I look up?   No pins.

Guiding balls toward empty goals.

Pressing forward now out of spite.

Lonely and haunted by the ghosts of my visions.

HAPPY NEW YEAR, AND GOD BLESS

New year new me
Old year old me
Old yeller dead meat
Hot action hot feet
Muss and fuss
Cuss a bunch
Old day same shit
New shit never change
New pants new pleat
Cold action cold hands
Bust a nut
Do some sus
New night old shit
Old shit loose change
New range old flame
Fresh day start again

PRAYER FOR
A HAPPY LIFE

Do better
Try harder
Do better
Try harder
Do better
Try harder
Do better
Try harder

TWAS THE NIGHT BEFORE TOMORROW

We laid down for winter's nap
Cold and dark had sapped our sap
Not a kerchief or a cap
In sight
Just two people living in the moment

I don't recall the last time I was asleep by ten.

I dreamt of our savior
It's weird to dream about technology

COME WITH ME IF YOU WANT TO LIVE

Happy birthday, Baby Jee
Three wise men came to see
You will live to 33
Then get stapled to a tree
But you'll get likes and follows plenty
Through bap' and conf' and euch' and repenty

Happy birthday Baby God
You turned water into grog
At 3 and 30 stapled to a log
You cast from temple for money lent
But forgot the priests were charging rent
2000 years later tax exempt

Happy birthday Micro Jesus
Your boi Pontius failed to please us
30 plus 3, that year was junk
You got stapled to a trunk
Now most your flock more sheep than before
Instead of false golden calf its orange rich boor

Happy birthday JHC
Undeafed the deaf and made blindies see
33rd was tacked to some wood
Then Judas swung from a branch
And you beat death in a boxing match
I don't believe but I like your panache

Happy birthday King of Jews
Mary Mags was your boo
3 times 11 was all it'd be,
stapled roughly to a T
You did good in the face of spite
Emulating you is, I think, right
Even though I don't pray to you at night

BUT YOU AIN'T ME

Ain't no good
To go on a rant
If you could you should
If you can't you can't
If you can you can
If you shan't you shan't
If you spend the coin
What's spent is spant
If you can dance the dance
Then sport the pant
If you have two legs
Pluralize to pants
If you have a third leg
Then you'd be Max

BOTTOM

If you show up in joots and jorts
I will serve you finest tort

If you run by in matching track suit
I will serve you marrow and suet

If you sport a cap while making haste
I will serve you turkey's baste

If you make haste while sporting cap
I will serve you milk from tap

If you beat tracks whilst donning jeans
I will serve you richest creams

If you come hither wearing Spanx
I will serve you roasted shanks

If you arrive in sportsman's coat
I will serve you banana float

PUMA DOESN'T CARE ABOUT YOUR FEEBLE ATTEMPTS TO SLEEP

Four straight days on E
The kind of E you can only achieve
Through unsafe ingestion of caffeine
Levels beyond reason to get through 18 hours
Levels so high you then lay awake perpetually
Feeling life drain out of your pores
The way an 18 wheeler's jake brake starts hot
Then tapers
Or the way it takes a pot a while to boil
Before vapors
After three straight days of running on fumes
A fourth where every feeling is intensifying doom
Now reacting like a child
Not with wonder but vitriol and bile
Then when you finally lie down to rest the head
At four AM the cat pukes on the bed

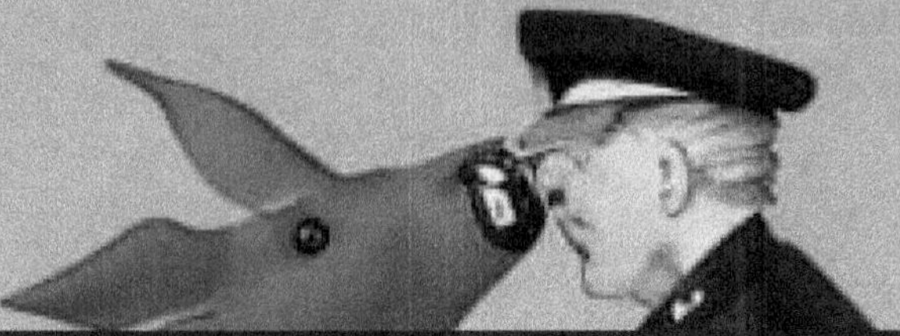

WHAT IS THIS? A CROSSOVER EPISODE?

Here comes Donald
Here comes Donald
Right down Pennsylvania lane
Locking up foreign girls and boys and laughing at their pain
Grabbing a pussy, eating a Big Mac, telling tremendous lies
So gird your loins and grease your skids
Cause Donald is coming tonight

Or, if you don't like that, how about.......

Whistles blow, are you listening?
On foreheads, sweat is glistening
A beautiful sight
Tell tremendous lies
Walking in an impeachment wonderland

Gone away, is decorum
No civility in this forum
Talk about puss
On a hot mike with Billy Bush
Walking in an impeachment wonderland

In the south Trump can build a border wall
In an attempt to keep out all the browns
When we ask him who will pay
He'll say Mexico!
But we know that's a fucking lie because he's a liar and I know this isn't how the song goes but here we are

THE COST OF DOING BUSINESS

Set off this bomb with aplomb:
We can measure time, but can we weigh it?
When it's you v. me
Who's to say which 3:33 P
Is more valuable?
Should we all go by billable rates?
Is it dollars and cents?
Is it post-encounter time spent
To remember or forget?
Forgetting has more cost
But who pays?
I'll be levying that tax for days;
That same experience for you
Might equal sipping lemonade in the shade.
If you act like my time is worth less
Then you better be on your best!
I'll not front the funds for that transaction
Too much of that behavior elicits capital passion.

BOOT(HILL) SCOOT AND BOOGIE

Some days are worse
Others worse still
But being alive
Is preferred to Boot Hill
You can eat right
You can go to bed
It all ends the same
Dead dead dead
Xs for eyes
Dust where once skin
When your life is over
Someone else's begins
You can swing in the barn
Or make hay in the sack
But once these minutes tick by
There's no going back

AND HE SHOOK WHEN
HE LAUGHED LIKE A BOWL
FULL OF SOUP

People who say you've got a case of the Mondays
Need pushed down the stairs
But I've got a case of the Mondays
Every day of the week this time of year
Ma in her kerchief
Me with my sap
Santa can GFHS
How about that?

SAMETWO NOTES IN THIS (RIP)CHORD

The thing about self-awareness
Is that it's only as valuable as your last fuck-up
To have only a modicum of self-worth to begin with
Then have that little glimmer
Spiked on the concrete……
Why even finish this poem?
Why even go home?
Riding the coattails of a lie
Everything once thought working
Just poked you in the eye
And if your best is exposed as fraudulent?
Pretty easy at this point to pack it in
Hard to recharge the juice
Hard to force a grin

GET ME OFF
THIS PICTURE

A trisket a trasket
Put the lotion in the basket
I went to town to call my love
But the phone line was down
So I left town and headed on around
To the next town where the water was brown
And I drank some of that water and got pink eye
And pink throat and pink everything
and the saw bones said he'd have to take my leg
And I bit down on a spoon
While some poor man's Billy Joel
Played a tired tune at the local saloon
Then we buried my leg in a sand dune
And saved the rest of me for boot hill
And now instead of running anywhere
I just stand still

DISDAIN

I'm not his elixir
I'm not his cure
It's not my responsibility
To keep his head clear
I'm not his service dog
I'm not his therapy blanket
I'm will never be his punching bag
Nor his fodder when he cranks it
It's not fair to place me
On some pedestal of glass
Like I'm some miracle cure
When he acts like an ass
How narcissistic!
How manipulative!
How vain!
To try to make me the cure to his pain
Work on himself
That's what he should do
Before forcing me into a responsibility
That I don't want to do
I'm not his elixir
I'm not his cure
If he isn't carefully
I won't even be here

I, DUMB ASS

I didn't realize
When I was a child
That even though my life would be an adventure
It is really just
Filling in the gaps
Between times I have to do
The dishes

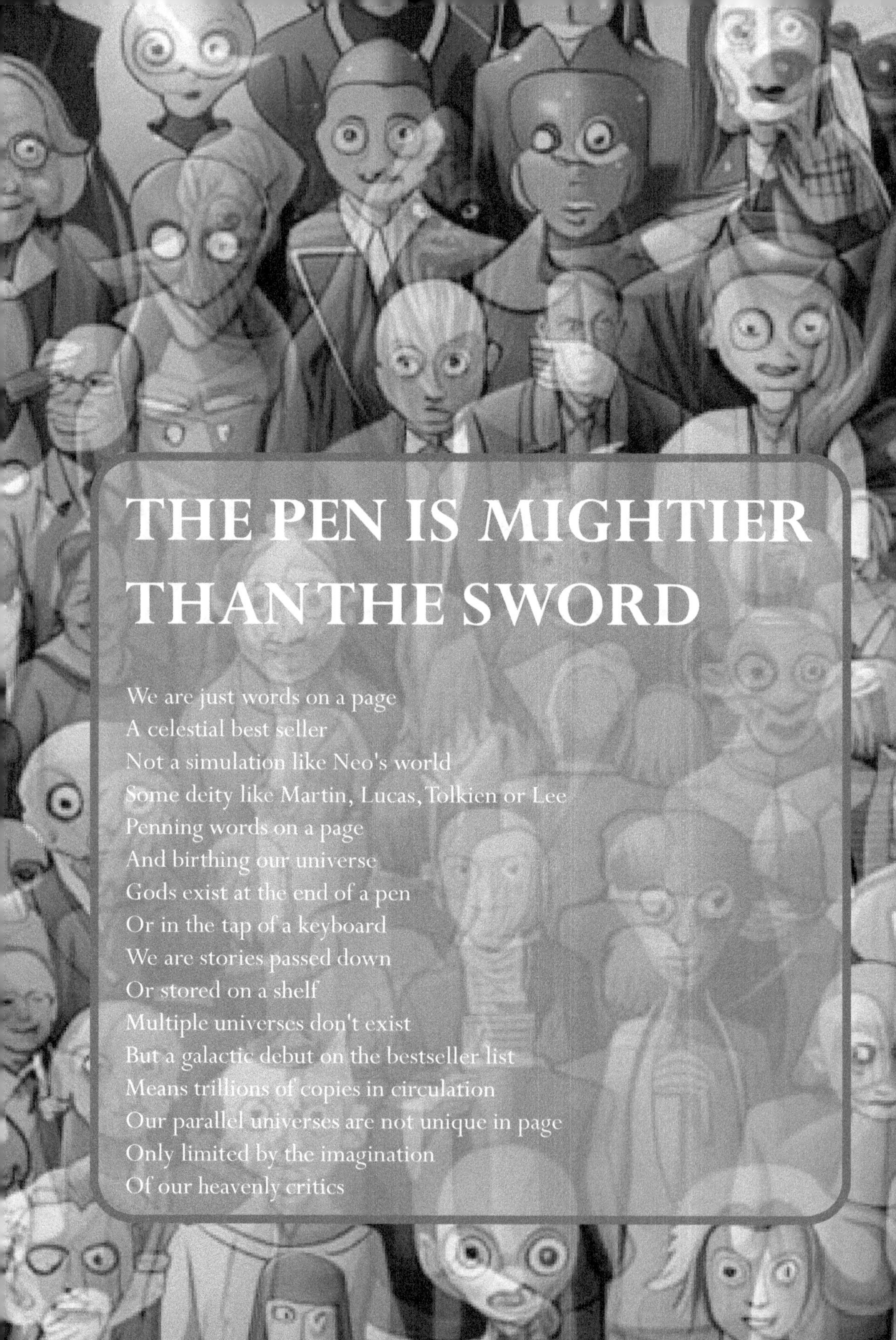

THE PEN IS MIGHTIER THAN THE SWORD

We are just words on a page
A celestial best seller
Not a simulation like Neo's world
Some deity like Martin, Lucas, Tolkien or Lee
Penning words on a page
And birthing our universe
Gods exist at the end of a pen
Or in the tap of a keyboard
We are stories passed down
Or stored on a shelf
Multiple universes don't exist
But a galactic debut on the bestseller list
Means trillions of copies in circulation
Our parallel universes are not unique in page
Only limited by the imagination
Of our heavenly critics

THIS NIGHT WILL NEVER HAPPEN AGAIN

Made a mistake
Stayed up too late
Tucked you in
About to sleep
And then I felt the
Motivation creep
This is my devil
This is my curse
1 AM drive is
The fucking dirt-worst
I should be sleeping
I should be out cold
Tomorrow is here, now
And I am so wound
But I have to make hay
While the Sun shows her face
Because if I don't?
What if these words escape?
What if I don't get it on tape?
What if I die in my sleep?

And you never know how I truly feel.
And you never know that I think I stole
The best years of your life
I am eternally sorry for my behavior
Age 23 to this morning, or later
But I love you so god damned much
It causes physical pain
Any time I think I've driven a wedge
Any time I feel the feelings wane
But like just after a new moon, tomorrow I'm back
That's only four hours from now
But I'll get through it somehow
I may need to hold your hand
And feel your skin against mine
I hope some small part of you
Feels the same
But I hope you feel it without the self-blame
This 2 AM impulse
How I know I'm not in a simulation
Because words this honest cannot come from some
machination
Rest easy tonight while I bang out these thoughts
Tomorrow's a new day, and luckily, we have a full coffee pot

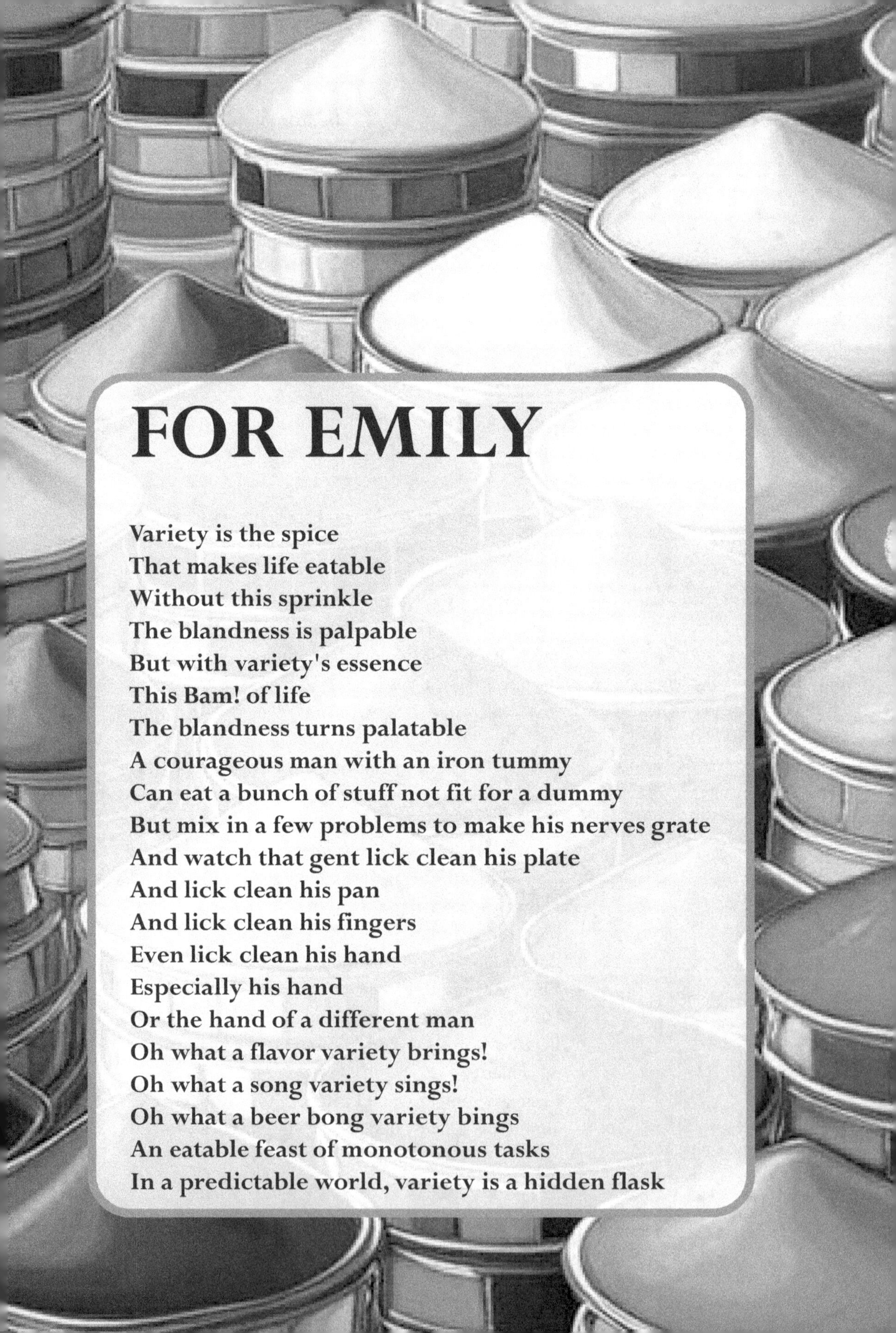

FOR EMILY

Variety is the spice
That makes life eatable
Without this sprinkle
The blandness is palpable
But with variety's essence
This Bam! of life
The blandness turns palatable
A courageous man with an iron tummy
Can eat a bunch of stuff not fit for a dummy
But mix in a few problems to make his nerves grate
And watch that gent lick clean his plate
And lick clean his pan
And lick clean his fingers
Even lick clean his hand
Especially his hand
Or the hand of a different man
Oh what a flavor variety brings!
Oh what a song variety sings!
Oh what a beer bong variety bings
An eatable feast of monotonous tasks
In a predictable world, variety is a hidden flask

Every foul is not a flagrant
Less than a ten in your pocket?
That makes you a vagrant
Make your point in less than ten words?
That means you are salient
Throw that brick through the foyer wall?
That makes you an assailant
Share an electron with a friendly face?
That makes you covalent
Live in a house owned by another?
That means you are paying rent
Flagrant vagrant?
Salient assailant?
Covalent paying rent?
What was this? A crossover episode?

PLAY THE CARDS

You can't plan for a pandemic, and you shouldn't. All you can do is react. Today was meant to be our wedding day, but instead we tubed down the Yellow River in anticipation of next year. In a time of post Covid. Punting the wedding doesn't mean we love each other less. It means we love others more than our own events. So we made hay while the sun shined. We made lemonade out of life's lemons that it continues to throw at us, even today. But that's just fine with me, because my sweetheart can soften the bite of any lemon. Together, we are more. So today we tubed a river instead of having a wedding, and next year we'll have a wedding instead of something else.

And in between we'll drink lemonade.

Follow Me Here:

@yesterdayinpoetry
@holdforswank
@promptmax

If you made it this far,
thanks, and I'm sorry.